Mormon Wisdom

Mormon Wisdom

Inspirational Sayings from Latter-day Saints

Compiled and Introduced by
Christopher Kimball Bigelow, Bennett
Floyd, and Jonathan Langford

Skyhorse Publishing

Copyright © 2015 by Skyhorse Publishing

Skyhorse Publishing books may be purchased in bulk at special discounts for sales promotion, corporate gifts, fund-raising, or educational purposes. Special editions can also be created to specifications. For details, contact the Special Sales Department, Skyhorse Publishing, 307 West 36th Street, 11th Floor, New York, NY 10018 or info@skyhorsepublishing.com.

Skyhorse® and Skyhorse Publishing® are registered trademarks of Skyhorse Publishing, Inc.®, a Delaware corporation.

Visit our website at www.skyhorsepublishing.com.

10 9 8 7 6 5 4 3 2 1

Library of Congress Cataloging-in-Publication Data is available on file.

Cover design by Brian Peterson
Cover photo credit: Thinkstock

Print ISBN: 978-1-63220-635-0
Ebook ISBN: 978-1-63220-791-3

Printed in China.

Contents

INTRODUCTION

It's hard to imagine Mexican or Italian food without tomatoes. What would traditional, homemade spaghetti be without a rich marinara sauce? Or a plate of warm nachos without some tangy pico de gallo? As versatile as the tomato may be, however, it has its limitations. Ask a child to bite into a ripe tomato, and her face will not likely register pleasure. As British journalist Miles Kington noted, "Knowledge consists of knowing that a tomato is a fruit, and wisdom consists of not putting it in a fruit salad."

The reality of life is that at some point or other, we all face our share of sweet and bitter times—some of us more than our fair share. Since its humble beginnings in 1830, Mormonism has seen its share of trials and opposition. Today, however, Mormons seem to have largely found their places in society, and the faith has taken its place among some of the world's most influential religions. Over time, Mormons have learned some valuable, distinctive lessons about the human experience, from how to maximize physical health to how to enjoy successful marriages and families.

WISDOM FROM THE MORMONS

This book collects wise sayings by a variety of Mormons, from Lucy Mack Smith, mother of founding prophet Joseph Smith, to leaders who only recently departed from this life. We chose not to include quotes from living people in order to avoid stepping on anyone's toes. This book is not an official LDS Church publication, and not all quotes reflect official Church doctrine. At the end of this volume, we've included brief bios on all those quoted.

We would have liked to find more quotes by
female LDS leaders.

Also included are quotations from Mormonism's unique scriptures, including the
Book of Mormon, the Doctrine & Covenants, and the Pearl of Great Price. As Christians, Mormons uphold the Bible as an equally
sacred, vital scripture. For this book, however,
we've opted to leave out Bible passages that
are no doubt already familiar to most readers.
Although other religious groups exist with ties
to historical Mormonism, this book focuses on
wisdom from members of the largest Mormon
faith, the Utah-based Church of Jesus Christ of
Latter-day Saints (LDS).

Many of the people quoted in this book are
past prophets, apostles, and other leaders of
the LDS Church. Perhaps one of the Church's
most unique features is its lack of professional
clergy, even at the highest levels of leadership.
While these men and women gained much
experience during their lives in leading and

inspiring the Church, most also pursued secular careers before serving in the Church full time, working in fields such as farming, business, teaching, politics, and many others. Nearly all of them married and had children. The wisdom collected in this volume was born not only of yearnings to understand the divine, but also of practical, earthly experience.

"WE SEEK AFTER THESE THINGS"

Mormons do not claim a monopoly on truth. One of the basic tenets of Mormon belief affirms, "If there is anything virtuous, lovely, or of good report, or praiseworthy, we seek after these things." Goodness, virtue, and edification can be found almost anywhere, if one is willing to search for it. Former Church president Gordon B. Hinckley (1910–2008) said to members in Nairobi, Kenya, "We appreciate the truth in all churches and the good which they do. We say to the people, in effect, you bring with you all the good that you have, and then let us see if we can add to it."

Mormonism provides unique insights on where we came from, why we're here, and where we're going. Whether one is a lifelong Mormon, a convert to Mormonism, a member of another faith, or not a participant in organized religion, it's our hope that the gems of wisdom collected in this volume may provide food for thought—and maybe a smile or two.

Like members of other faiths, Mormons are continually striving to understand our true identities as children of God, be faithful to God's teachings, and serve God and our fellow brothers and sisters. Not unlike a good cookbook that tells you when and how to include tomatoes in your dish, we trust that this collection of Mormon wisdom will inform, inspire, and elevate your life and the lives of those around you.

HEAVENLY PARENTS

Where do we come from? The answer to this question has been hotly debated by some of the world's greatest philosophers, scientists, and thinkers. Many religions, particularly Abrahamic faiths, teach that God is our father, a loving, all-powerful, and all-knowing being who created us and placed us on Earth for a specific purpose. These faiths generally share the understanding that life, for humans, begins at birth.

However, Mormonism claims a unique perspective among its religious peers. Like members of other churches, Latter-day Saints believe that God is the spiritual father of humankind. They commonly refer to him as "Heavenly Father," addressing him as such during prayer. Unlike other faiths, Mormon doctrine teaches that everyone—Mormon and non-Mormon alike—lived with Heavenly Father *before* earthly birth, a period of time commonly referred to by Mormons as "premortality" or "the premortal life."

In addition, Latter-day Saints are taught that God is not a single parent. We not only have a father in heaven, but also a mother. For cultural reasons, Mormons rarely mention Heavenly Mother, but the understanding that each of us has a divine parentage can profoundly shape our view of life and its purpose (see **Divine Potential; Purpose of Life**).

—⁂—

In the premortal realm, spirit sons and daughters knew and worshipped God as their Eternal Father and accepted his plan by which his children could obtain a physical body and gain earthly experience to progress toward perfection and ultimately realize their divine destiny as heirs of eternal life.

—*The Family: A Proclamation to the World* (1995)

Nothing is going to startle us more when we pass through the veil to the other side than to realize how well we know our Father and how familiar his face is to us.

—*Ezra Taft Benson* (1899–1994)

All human beings—male and female—are created in the image of God. Each is a beloved spirit son or daughter of heavenly parents, and, as such, each has a divine nature and destiny.

—*The Family: A Proclamation to the World* (1995)

In the heav'ns are parents single?
No, the thought makes reason stare!
Truth is reason; truth eternal
Tells me I've a mother there.

When I leave this frail existence,
When I lay this mortal by,
Father, Mother, may I meet you
In your royal courts on high?
　　　　　　　—Eliza R. Snow (1804–1877)

All men and women are in the similitude of the universal Father and Mother and are literally the sons and daughters of Deity.... Man, as a spirit, was begotten and born of heavenly parents, and reared to maturity in the eternal mansions of the Father, prior to coming upon the earth in a temporal body to undergo an experience in mortality.... Man is the child of God, formed in the divine image and endowed with divine attributes.

　　　　　　　　　　—*The Origin of Man*
(First Presidency statement, 1909)

I am a child of God,
And he has sent me here,
Has given me an earthly home
With parents kind and dear.
　　　　　—Naomi W. Randall (1908–2001)

God truly is our Father, the Father of the spirits of all mankind. We are his literal offspring and are formed in his image. We have inherited divine characteristics from him. Knowing our relationship to our Heavenly Father helps us understand the divine nature that is in us and our potential.

　　　　　—Joseph B. Wirthlin (1917–2008)

It doesn't take from our worship of the Eternal Father, to adore our Eternal Mother, any more than it diminishes the love we bear our earthly fathers, to include our earthly mothers in our affections.

　　　　　—Rudger Clawson (1857–1943)

There can be no God except he is composed of the man and woman united, and there is not in all the eternities that exist, or ever will be a God in any other way.

—Erastus Snow (1818–1888)

Sometimes we think the whole job is up to us, forgetful that there are loved ones beyond our sight who are thinking about us and our children. We forget that we have a Heavenly Father and a Heavenly Mother who are even more concerned, probably, than our earthly father and mother, and that influences from beyond are constantly working to try to help us when we do all we can.

—Harold B. Lee (1899–1973)

In accordance with gospel philosophy there are males and females in heaven. Since we have a Father, who is our God, we must also have a mother, who possesses the attributes of godhood. This simply carries onward the logic of things earthly, and conforms with the doctrine that whatever is on this earth is simply a representation of great spiritual conditions of deeper meaning than we can here fathom.

—John A. Widtsoe (1872–1952)

DIVINE
POTENTIAL

One of the most distinctive Mormon teachings is that as literal sons and daughters of heavenly parents, humans have innate divine potential. Just as earthly parents want their children to grow up, become adults, and ultimately have families of their own, the ultimate purpose of creation, in the Mormon view, is for us to become like our heavenly parents (see **Heavenly Parents**).

This puts a unique perspective on many aspects of the gospel message. Obedience to God's commandments, for example, is seen not only as an act of reverence to God, but also as following precepts that God has established in order for us to become like him (see **Obedience**).

Similarly, the life and mission of Jesus Christ take on added meaning as opening up a path that allows us as humans to cast off our sins and fulfill our divine nature.

Generally there is in man a divinity which strives to push him onward and upward. We believe that this power within him is the spirit that comes from God. Man lived before he came to this earth, and he is here now to strive to perfect the spirit within.

—David O. McKay (1873–1970)

If men do not comprehend the character of God, they do not comprehend themselves.

—Joseph Smith (1805–1844)

Even as the infant son of an earthly father and mother is capable in due time of becoming a man, so the undeveloped offspring of celestial parentage is capable, by experience through ages and aeons, of evolving into a God.

—*The Origin of Man*
(First Presidency statement, 1909)

"To be or not to be?" That is not the question. What is the question? The question is not one of being, but of becoming. "To become more or not to become more." This is the question faced by each intelligence in our universe.

—Truman G. Madsen (1926–2009)

The idea is not to do good because of the praise of men; but to do good because in doing good we develop godliness within us, and this being the case we shall become allied to godliness, which will in time become part and portion of our being.

—Lorenzo Snow (1814–1901)

An intelligent being, in the image of God, possesses every organ, attribute, sense, sympathy, affection, of will, wisdom, love, power and gift, which is possessed by God himself. But these are possessed by man, in his rudimental state, in a subordinate sense of the word. Or, in other words, these attributes are in embryo; and are to be gradually developed. They resemble a bud—a germ, which gradually develops into bloom, and then, by progress, produces the mature fruit, after its own kind.

—Parley P. Pratt (1807–1857)

Even the person you think the worst off—and in some cases that may be yourself—even that personality that it has been most difficult for you to forgive will be, in a century or two, in such a condition that if you saw him or her your first impulse would be to kneel in reverence. The truth is that the embryo within the worst of us is divine.

—Truman G. Madsen (1926–2009)

It is the first principle of the gospel to know for a certainty the character of God, and to know that we may converse with him as one man converses with another, and that he was once a man like us; yea, that God himself, the Father of us all, dwelt on an earth.

—Joseph Smith (1805–1844)

As man now is, God once was; as God is now, man may be.

—Lorenzo Snow (1814–1901)

Gender is an essential characteristic of individual premortal, mortal, and eternal identity and purpose.
—*The Family: A Proclamation to the World* (1995)

I am perfectly satisfied that my Father and my god is a cheerful, pleasant, lively, and good-natured Being. Why? Because I am cheerful, pleasant, lively, and good-natured when I have his Spirit. . . . That arises from the perfection of his attributes; he is a jovial, lively person, and a beautiful man.

—Heber C. Kimball (1801–1868)

We are daughters of our Heavenly Father, who loves us, and we love him. We will "stand as witnesses of God at all times and in all things, and in all places" (Mosiah 18:9) as we strive to live the Young Women values, which are: Faith, Divine Nature, Individual Worth, Knowledge, Choice and Accountability, Good Works, Integrity, and Virtue. We believe as we come to accept and act upon these values, we will be prepared to strengthen home and family, make and keep sacred covenants, receive the ordinances of the temple, and enjoy the blessings of exaltation.

—Young Women theme (2010)

God's very nature requires that he should have peers.

—Truman G. Madsen (1926–2009)

God himself was once as we are now, and is an exalted man, and sits enthroned in yonder heavens! That is the great secret. If the veil were rent today, and the great God who holds this world in its orbit, and who upholds all worlds and all things by his power, was to make himself visible—I say, if you were to see him today, you would see him like a man in form—like yourselves in all the person, image, and very form as a man; for Adam was created in the very fashion, image and likeness of God, and received instruction from, and walked, talked and conversed with him, as one man talks and communes with another.

—Joseph Smith (1805–1844)

At the end of this process, our Heavenly Parents will have sons and daughters who are their peers, their friends, and their colleagues.

—Chieko N. Okazaki (1926–2011)

CREATION

For members of the LDS Church, the Creation wasn't a magical event. God didn't "poof" humanity, the world, and the universe into existence. In fact, for Mormons the term *creation* is something of a misnomer. God's role in the Creation is not unlike that of an architect. With the help of his Son, Jesus Christ, God used his knowledge of natural laws and elements already in existence to design and organize our world and everything in it. Together, they created physical human bodies, into which they placed the spirits of Adam and Eve, who would become the primordial predecessors of all humankind (see **Heavenly Parents; Divine Potential**).

Whether this process of creation took six literal days, as the Bible suggests, or billions of years as scientists claim, LDS leaders offer no clear answers. The Church likewise has no official position on the theory of evolution. What Mormons agree on, however, is that no matter what the specifics, God, our all-knowing and all-powerful father, and his Son, Jesus Christ, organized and created our world—and countless others—for us to enjoy and appreciate and so that we might return to live with them (see **Purpose of Life**).

—⚊—

I was early taught . . . to love that Being, who has made the earth so beautiful, and provided so much for his creatures dwelling thereon; thus I was early led to admire and reverence the Creator through his works.

—Hannah Last Cornaby (1822–1905)

Now, the word *create* . . . does not mean to create out of nothing; it means to organize; the same as a man would organize materials and build a ship. Hence, we infer that God had materials to organize the world out of chaos.

—Joseph Smith (1805–1844)

The earth, as a part of the creation of God, has fulfilled and will fulfill the measure of its creation. It has been baptized by water, it will be baptized by fire; it will be purified and become celestial, and be a fit place for celestial bodies to inhabit.

—John Taylor (1808–1887)

The fulness of the earth is yours, the beasts of the field and the fowls of the air, and that which climbeth upon the trees and walketh upon the earth;

Yea, and the herb, and the good things which come of the earth, whether for food or for raiment, or for houses, or for barns, or for orchards, or for gardens, or for vineyards;

Yea, all things which come of the earth, in the season thereof, are made for the benefit and the use of man, both to please the eye and to gladden the heart;

Yea, for food and for raiment, for taste and for smell, to strengthen the body and to enliven the soul.

And it pleaseth God that he hath given all these things unto man; for unto this end were they made to be used, with judgment, not to excess, neither by extortion.

—Doctrine & Covenants 59:16–20

However infinite the variety of its changes, forms and shapes; . . . eternity is inscribed in indelible characters on every particle.

—Parley P. Pratt (1807–1857)

God created all things. Nothing came by chance, but rather by his will and pleasure, his planning and knowledge, his power and love. The universe, in its infinite variety of life, testifies of his infinite intelligence, power, and majesty. And we, who want to know the meaning of it all, are reassured, not merely by the words, but by the whisperings of the Spirit that divine intelligence ordered all of it: by the power of his word, they were created.

—Keith Meservy (1924–2008)

The difference between God and the devil is that God creates and organizes, while the whole study of the devil is to destroy.

—Brigham Young (1801–1877)

Life existed long before our solar system was called into being. The fact is, there never was a time when man—made in the image of God, male and female—did not exist . . . . The Lord has given us the information regarding his creations, and how he has made many earths, for there never was a beginning, never was a time when man did not exist somewhere in the universe, and when the time came for this earth to be peopled, the Lord, our God, transplanted upon it from some other earth, the life which is found here.

—Joseph Fielding Smith (1876–1972)

There is life in all matter, throughout the vast extent of all eternities; it is in the rock, the sand, the dust, in water, air, the gases, and, in short, in every description and organization of matter, whether it be solid, liquid, or gaseous, particle operating with particle.

—Brigham Young (1801–1877)

Nature is the glass reflecting God, as by the sea reflected is the sun, too glorious to be gazed on in his sphere.

—Brigham Young (1801–1877)

The spirit of man is not a created being; it existed from eternity, and will exist to eternity.

—Joseph Smith (1805–1844)

There is no such thing as immaterial matter. All spirit is matter, but it is more fine or pure, and can only be discerned by purer eyes; we cannot see it; but when our bodies are purified we shall see that it is all matter.

—Doctrine & Covenants 131:7–8

Any theory that leaves out God as a personal, purposeful Being, and accepts chance as a first cause, cannot be accepted.... That man and the whole of creation came by chance is unthinkable. It is equally unthinkable that if man came into being by the will and power of God, the divine creative power is limited to one process dimly sensed by mortal man.

—John A. Widtsoe (1872–1952)

PURPOSE OF LIFE

What is the meaning of life? Does life have meaning? Latter-day Saints are not the first to tackle these questions, but they offer answers somewhat different from those commonly provided by other Christian religions.

According to Mormon doctrine, life is merely a step toward our goal of becoming like our heavenly parents, a brief moment in our eternal progression. It's designed to be a test, a trial of whether or not we will exercise our faith and free will (see **Choices & Freedom**) to follow God's commandments and prove worthy to return to him after death through our obedience (see **Obedience**). In addition, Mormons believe that this test is one that we all freely chose to undergo in the premortal world (see **Heavenly Parents; Divine Potential**).

For Mormons, this test isn't necessarily meant to be easy. Each of us must pass through significant challenges and adversity (see **Trials**). With this adversity also comes the blessing of a clearer sense of purpose and a hope that, although life may be hard, it can nonetheless be enjoyed, knowing that bumps or bruises gained along the way will be worth it.

—⁊⁊⁊—

This life is not given to us as a pastime. There was a solemn purpose in our creation, in the life that God has given to us. Let us study what that purpose is, that we may progress and obtain eternal life.

—George Albert Smith (1870–1951)

I believe that every person who is called to do an important work in the kingdom of God was called to that work or was foreordained to that work before this world was.

—Joseph Smith (1805–1844)

There was a space granted unto man in which he might repent; therefore this life became a probationary state; a time to prepare to meet God; a time to prepare for that endless state which has been spoken of by us, which is after the resurrection of the dead.

—Book of Mormon, Alma 12:24

Now the Lord had shown unto me, Abraham, the intelligences that were organized before the world was; and among all these there were many of the noble and great ones;

And God saw these souls that they were good . . . and he said unto me: Abraham, thou art one of them; thou wast chosen before thou wast born.

—Pearl of Great Price, Abraham 3:22–23

Man is spirit. The elements are eternal, and spirit and element, inseparably connected, receive a fulness of joy.

—Doctrine & Covenants 93:33

One of the main purposes of our existence is that we might conform to the image and likeness of him who sojourned in the flesh without blemish—immaculate, pure and spotless! Christ came not only to atone for the sins of the world, but to set an example before all men and to establish the standard of God's perfection, of God's law, and of obedience to the Father.

—Joseph F. Smith (1838–1919)

If we are striving, if we are working, if we are trying, to the best of our ability, to improve day by day, then we are in the line of our duty.

—Heber J. Grant (1856–1945)

We may have given to us, in this life, a few things that will give us satisfaction, temporally; but the things that are eternal, the things that are worthwhile, are those eternal things that we reach out for, and prepare ourselves to receive, and lay hold of by the effort that we individually make.

—George Albert Smith (1870–1951)

It is glorious when you can lie down at night with a clear conscience, knowing you have done your best not to offend anyone and have injured no man. You have tried to cleanse your heart of all unrighteousness, and if you put forth precious effort, you can sense as you pray to God to keep you that night that he accepts your effort. You have a sense that you are God's child, not a mere cog of the state, but a person whose soul God wants to save. You have the strength, the sense of resistance to evil. . . . You also have the realization that you have made the world better for having been in it

—David O. McKay (1873–1970)

Any conduct on the part of an individual that does not advance him toward the goal of eternal life is not only wasted energy but actually becomes the basis of sin.

—Harold B. Lee (1899–1973)

Jesus Christ has laid out a plan for us which will bring us and our loved ones eternal life if we are faithful. That life will be a busy, purposeful life with accomplishments and joys and development.

—Spencer W. Kimball (1895–1985)

Life is not accumulation, it is about contribution.

—Stephen R. Covey (1932–2012)

We came to this earth that we might have a body and present it pure before God. . . . The great principle of happiness consists in having a body.

—Joseph Smith (1805–1844)

Men, discouraged by their failure to accomplish exactly what they desire, often speak of their lives as purposeless, but it is idle talk, for, in fact, no intelligent life which concerns itself vigorously and properly with the things about it can be said to be purposeless. . . . The only purposeless life is the one that does not use its faculties. It matters little what tasks men perform in life, if only they do them well and with all their strength.

—John A. Widtsoe (1872–1952)

TRIALS

If God is truly a loving, all-knowing, and all-powerful being, how can he possibly allow so much suffering? The Mormon answer to this question is complex and will perhaps be dissatisfying to some, but it may nonetheless provide valuable insight to those undergoing difficult times.

Mormons generally believe that no suffering is completely without meaning or purpose. Like a parent who takes his or her child to the doctor for shots, God allows us to endure fear, uncertainty, pain, discomfort, and hardship for our ultimate good. Our trials are designed to help us—and others within our sphere of influence—to grow, whether such growth is physical, mental, or spiritual in nature.

Some trials are inflicted upon us by the choices of others or ourselves. Some come by accident. According to Mormon teachings, God gives each person the gift of free will (see **Choices & Freedom**). God so values this gift that he will not generally remove the natural consequences of anyone's actions, even if such consequences may cause intense suffering.

Whether trials come on their own or as the result of choices, we are encouraged to endure our trials well. The blessings of exaltation and eternal life await all who do.

—⚏—

Oh, how I suffered of cold and hunger and the keenest of all was to hear my little ones crying for bread, and I had none to give them; but in all the Lord was with us and gave us grace and faith to stand it all.

—Jane Elizabeth Manning James (1822–1908)

Trials and tribulations tend to squeeze the artificiality out of us, leaving the essence of what we really are and clarifying what we really yearn for.

—Neal A. Maxwell (1926–2004)

We have got to be tried and proved in all things so that we may stand or fall.

—Ann Marsh Abbott (1797–1849)

I don't believe that faith means God will remove all tragedies from our path or solve all of our problems for us. I believe it means that he will be with us, suffering with us and grieving with us and working with us as we deal with our own tragedies and work our way through our problems.

—Chieko N. Okazaki (1926–2011)

At such times when we feel the floods are threatening to drown us and the deep is going to swallow up the tossed vessel of our faith, I pray we may always hear amid the storm and the darkness that sweet utterance of the Savior of the world: "Be of good cheer: it is I; be not afraid" (Matt. 14:27).

—Howard W. Hunter (1907–1995)

To never doubt that [Heavenly Father] guides the details of our lives, to be able in life's conflict to say "Thy will be done," is the attaining of the ability to walk by faith. This ability is something that each soul must find in his own way through the creative living out of any and all trying experiences that may come along.

—Stella Harris Oaks (1906–1980)

Peace be unto thy soul; thine adversity and thine afflictions shall be but a small moment; and then, if thou endure it well, God shall exalt thee on high.

—Doctrine & Covenants 121:7–8

While we sometimes feel, and have felt in days that are past and gone, to complain because we meet with oppression, persecution, and affliction, yet I wish to say to my brethren and sisters that these things are the heritage of the Saints of God. . . . I have never read of the people of God in any dispensation passing through life, as the sectarian world would say, on flowery beds of ease, without opposition of any kind.

—Wilford Woodruff (1807–1898)

Adversity is an important part of the preparation for at least three reasons. One, God knows whom he can trust and who, like Job, will stand firm and love him unconditionally. Second, adversity well handled can increase our understanding and compassion. And we will be more effective in helping others when we've had a few challenges of our own. We just may need to be an answer to somebody else's prayer. And third, we draw closer to our Heavenly Father when we are in deep need. Our prayers of thanksgiving and joy of course should be part, and are a part, of our worship, but I guess there isn't anybody here who won't admit that we pray more fervently when we're under the press of problems. Attitude in adversity turns hopeless to hopeful.

—Elaine A. Cannon (1922–2003)

Why face life's burdens alone, Christ asks, or why face them with temporal support that will quickly falter? To the heavy laden it is Christ's yoke, it is the power and peace of standing side by side with a God that will provide the support, balance, and the strength to meet our challenges and endure our tasks here in the hardpan field of mortality.

—Howard W. Hunter (1907–1995)

Adversity is frequently a call to do something great with our lives.

—Chieko N. Okazaki (1926–2011)

The Lord compensates the faithful for every loss. That which is taken away from those who love the Lord will be added unto them in his own way. While it may not come at the time we desire, the faithful will know that every tear today will eventually be returned a hundredfold with tears of rejoicing and gratitude.

—Joseph B. Wirthlin (1917–2008)

We are here that we may be educated in a school of suffering and of fiery trials, which school was necessary for Jesus our elder brother, who, the scriptures tell us, was made perfect through suffering. It is necessary we suffer in all things, that we may be qualified and worthy to rule and govern all things, even as our Father in heaven and his eldest son Jesus.

—Lorenzo Snow (1814–1901)

All experience is for our good because we learn in no other way.

—Chieko N. Okazaki (1926–2011)

Every trial a man goes through, if he is faithful in that trial and does honor to God and his religion he has espoused, at the end of that trial or affliction that individual is nearer to God, nearer in regard to the increase of faith, wisdom, knowledge, and power, and hence is more confident in calling upon the Lord for those things he desires.

—Lorenzo Snow (1814–1901)

May we be strengthened with the understanding that being blessed does not mean that we shall always be spared all the disappointments and difficulties of life.

—Heber J. Grant (1856–1945)

The loss of my beloved husband is the hardest thing that has ever happened to me. I am a triple cancer survivor. I have been near death three times from other causes. Those were testing times. Sometimes I thought I had been tested to the point of breaking. But none of them compares with the testing following Ed's death. There have been times when I literally could not turn the doorknob and leave the house without praying for strength and imploring the Lord for his Spirit to accompany me as I went out to perform my duties.

—Chieko N. Okazaki (1926–2011)

Never is the gospel of Jesus Christ more beautiful than in times of intense need, or in times of a severe storm within us as individuals, or in times of confusion and turmoil.

—Harold B. Lee (1899–1973)

Unfortunately, some of our greatest tribulations are the result of our own foolishness and weakness and occur because of our own carelessness or transgression.

—James E. Faust (1920–2007)

And if thou shouldst be cast into the pit, or into the hands of murderers, and the sentence of death passed upon thee; if thou be cast into the deep; if the billowing surge conspire against thee; if fierce winds become thine enemy; if the heavens gather blackness, and all the elements combine to hedge up the way; and above all, if the very jaws of hell shall gape open the mouth wide after thee, know thou, my son, that all these things shall give thee experience, and shall be for thy good.

—Doctrine & Covenants 122:7

Just as a floodlighted temple is more beautiful in a severe storm or in a heavy fog, so the gospel of Jesus Christ is more glorious in times of inward storm and of personal sorrow and tormenting conflict.

—Harold B. Lee (1899–1973)

It is well that we remember that the trials, difficulties, and experiences of life all have purpose. There came to me on the occasion of a year in my life to be remembered when the lovely sisters of our Relief Society wrote this as a prayer in my behalf. It was entitled "May You Have":

Enough happiness to keep you sweet,
Enough trials to keep you strong,
Enough sorrow to keep you human,
Enough hope to keep you happy,
Enough failure to keep you humble,
Enough success to keep you eager,
Enough wealth to meet your needs,
Enough enthusiasm to look forward,
Enough friends to give you comfort,
Enough faith to banish depression,
Enough determination to make each day better
    than yesterday.

This is my prayer for the faithful Saints in every land and throughout the world as we look forward to the future with courage and with fortitude.

—Harold B. Lee (1899–1973)

Just as we develop our physical muscles through overcoming opposition—such as lifting weights—we develop our character muscles by overcoming challenges and adversity.

—Stephen R. Covey (1932–2012)

If there were no night, we would not appreciate the day, nor could we see the stars and the vastness of the heavens. We must partake of the bitter with the sweet. There is a divine purpose in the adversities we encounter every day. They prepare, they purge, they purify, and thus they bless.

—James E. Faust (1920–2007)

All of us must face death—our own deaths and the deaths of loved ones. I feel that I am learning something about the way of the disciple that leads through the valley of the shadow of death, but even there—even there—I know I am following the Savior, and I can feel his hand upholding me and his voice promising me, "I will never leave thee, nor forsake thee" (Hebrews 13:5).

—Chieko N. Okazaki (1926–2011)

All your losses will be made up to you in the resurrection, provided you continue faithful. By the vision of the Almighty I have seen it.

—Joseph Smith (1805–1844)

All of us suffer some injuries from experiences that seem to have no rhyme or reason. We cannot understand or explain them. We may never know why some things happen in this life. The reason for some of our suffering is known only to the Lord.

—James E. Faust (1920–2007)

For it must needs be, that there is an opposition in all things. If not so, . . . righteousness could not be brought to pass, neither wickedness, neither holiness nor misery, neither good nor bad. Wherefore, all things must needs be a compound in one; wherefore, if it should be one body it must needs remain as dead, having no life neither death, nor corruption nor incorruption, happiness nor misery, neither sense nor insensibility.

—Book of Mormon, 2 Nephi 2:11

REPENTANCE
& FORGIVENESS

Most Christian denominations preach that salvation comes exclusively through the grace of Jesus Christ. LDS doctrine largely agrees, but it adds a caveat, as stated in the Book of Mormon: "for we know that it is by grace that we are saved, after all we can do" (2 Nephi 25:23). In other words, for Mormons mere confession of Jesus Christ as savior is not enough for salvation. Deathbed confessions do not do the trick. One must repent of his or her sins and strive diligently to keep God's commandments throughout life, repenting again and again as necessary.

Repentance, in the Mormon view, is an ongoing process. It may involve restitution to others we have wronged. In the case of serious sins, it may involve confession to Church leaders or civil authorities. It always involves "godly sorrow" for what we have done—not just sorrow that we have been caught, but true recognition that what we did was wrong. Repentance requires a lasting commitment to change. Ultimately, it should lead to internal change, as well as changes in external behavior.

Just as God commands us to repent, even so he promises us that true repentance will be rewarded with forgiveness. Forgiveness puts us right in our relationship to God and to our fellow human beings. It brings internal peace.

—ᴍ—

By this ye may know if a man repenteth of his sins—behold, he will confess them and forsake them.

—Doctrine & Covenants 58:43

Perfect people don't need a Savior. He came to save his people in their imperfections. He is the Lord of the living, and the living make mistakes. He's not embarrassed by us, angry at us, or shocked. He wants us in our brokenness, in our unhappiness, in our guilt and our grief.

—Chieko N. Okazaki (1926–2011)

And he cometh into the world that he may save all men if they will hearken unto his voice; for behold, he suffereth the pains of all men, yea, the pains of every living creature, both men, women, and children, who belong to the family of Adam.

—Book of Mormon, 2 Nephi 9:21

Some of our old traditions teach us that a man guilty of atrocious and murderous acts may savingly repent when on the scaffold; and upon his execution will hear the expression, "Bless God! He has gone to heaven, to be crowned in glory, through the all-redeeming merits of Christ the Lord." This is all nonsense. Such a character never will see heaven.

—Brigham Young (1801–1877)

Live out of your imagination, not your history.

—Stephen R. Covey (1932–2012)

You can always find somebody who is worse than you are to make you feel virtuous. It's a cheap shot: those awful terrorists, perverts, communists—they are the ones who need to repent! Yes, indeed they do, and for them repentance will be a full-time job, exactly as it is for all the rest of us.

—Hugh Nibley (1910–2005)

You cannot sink farther than the light and sweeping intelligence of Jesus Christ can reach. I bear testimony that as long as there is one spark of the will to repent and reach, he is there! He did not just descend to your condition, he descended below it; that he might be in and through all things the light of truth.

—Truman G. Madsen (1926–2009)

Never let a day pass that you will have cause to say, I will do better tomorrow.

—Brigham Young (1801–1877)

No man can sincerely resolve to apply to his daily life the teachings of Jesus of Nazareth without sensing a change in his own nature. The phrase "born again" has a deeper significance than many people attach to it. This changed feeling may be indescribable, but it is real.

—David O. McKay (1873–1970)

The purpose of the gospel is to make bad men good and good men better, and to change human nature.

—David O. McKay (1873–1970)

The heaviest burden that one has to bear in this life is the burden of sin.

—Harold B. Lee (1899–1973)

True repentance does not permit repetition.

—Spencer W. Kimball (1895–1985)

Self-justification is the enemy to repentance. God's spirit continues with the honest in heart to strengthen, to help, and to save, but invariably the Spirit of God ceases to strive with the man who "excuses" himself in his wrong doing.

—Spencer W. Kimball (1895–1985)

Godly sorrow is a gift of the Spirit.

—Ezra Taft Benson (1899–1994)

The Lord works from the inside out. The world works from the outside in. The world would take people out of the slums. Christ would take the slums out of people, and then they would take themselves out of the slums. The world would mold men by changing their environment. Christ changes men, who then change their environment. The world would shape human behavior, but Christ can change human nature.

—Ezra Taft Benson (1899–1994)

Men and women who turn their lives over to God will discover that he can make a lot more out of their lives than they can. He can deepen their joys, expand their vision, quicken their minds, strengthen their muscles, lift their spirits, multiply their blessings, increase their opportunities, comfort their souls, and pour out peace.

—Ezra Taft Benson (1899–1994)

True repentance involves a change of heart and not just a change of behavior.

—Ezra Taft Benson (1899–1994)

To those who have transgressed or been offended, we say, come back. The path of repentance, though hard at times, lifts one ever upward and leads to a perfect forgiveness.

—Howard W. Hunter (1907–1995)

As often as my people repent will I forgive them their trespasses against me. And ye shall also forgive one another your trespasses; for verily I say unto you, he that forgiveth not his neighbor's trespasses when he says that he repents, the same hath brought himself under condemnation.

—Book of Mormon, Mosiah 26:30–31

And if men come unto me I will show unto them their weakness. I give unto men weakness that they may be humble; and my grace is sufficient for all men that humble themselves before me; for if they humble themselves before me, and have faith in me, then will I make weak things become strong unto them.

—Book of Mormon, Ether 12:27

FAITH & SPIRITUALITY

It could be argued that the founding of the Church of Jesus Christ of Latter-day Saints came about all because of one simple question: "Which church should I join?" When he was only fourteen years old, Joseph Smith, the founder of Mormonism, knelt in prayer and asked God this very question, sincerely believing that he would receive an answer to his question. The rest, as they say, is history.

Faith, in the Mormon view, is more than just belief. Rather, it is belief that motivates to positive action, like the young Joseph kneeling to ask his question directly of God. As such, faith opens the gate to the influence of God's spirit. One of the fruits of righteous living is to enjoy the influence of that spirit in daily life. Ideally, spirituality becomes a way of life that influences our actions day by day.

—⁂—

If ye will awake and arouse your faculties, even to an experiment upon my words, and exercise a particle of faith, yea, even if ye can no more than desire to believe, let this desire work in you, even until ye believe in a manner that ye can give place for a portion of my words.

—Book of Mormon, Alma 32:27

Man is a spiritual being, a soul, and at some period of his life everyone is possessed with an irresistible desire to know his relationship to the Infinite. . . . There is something within him which urges him to rise above himself, to control his environment, to master the body and all things physical and live in a higher and more beautiful world.

—David O. McKay (1873–1970)

If I do not know the will of my Father, and what he requires of me in a certain transaction, if I ask him to give me wisdom concerning any requirement in my life, or in regard to my own course, or that of my friends, my family, my children, or those that I preside over, and get no answer from him, and then do the very best that my judgment will teach me, he is bound to own and honor that transaction, and he will do so to all intents and purposes.

—Brigham Young (1801–1877)

Let virtue garnish thy thoughts unceasingly; then shall thy confidence wax strong in the presence of God.

—Doctrine & Covenants 121:45

I only ask to go where the Lord would have me go, and only to receive what the Lord would have me receive, knowing that more important than sight is the witness that one may have by the witness of the Holy Ghost to his soul that things are so and that Jesus is the Christ, a living personage.

—Harold B. Lee (1899–1973)

Without faith you can do nothing.

—Doctrine & Covenants 8:10

There is a way by which persons can keep their consciences clear before God and man, and that is to preserve within them the Spirit of God, which is the spirit of revelation to every man and woman. It will reveal to them, even in the simplest of matters, what they shall do, by making suggestions to them. We should try to learn the nature of this spirit, that we may understand its suggestions, and then we will always be able to do right.

—Lorenzo Snow (1814–1901)

One fault to be avoided by the Saints, young and old, is the tendency to live on borrowed light [and] to permit . . . the light within them to be reflected, rather than original.

—Joseph F. Smith (1838–1919)

Spirituality is the consciousness of victory over self and communion with the infinite. Spirituality impels one to conquer difficulties and acquire more and more strength. To feel one's faculties unfolding and truth expanding the soul is one of life's sublimest experiences. Being true to self and being loyal to high ideals develops spirituality.

—David O. McKay (1873–1970)

There is a still small voice telling us what is right, and if we listen to that still small voice we shall grow and increase in strength and power, in testimony and in ability not only to live the gospel but to inspire others to do so. I value all things as nothing in comparison with having the spirit of God to guide me.

—Heber J. Grant (1856–1945)

We can live so we will have the whisperings of the good spirit all the time.

—Ann Prior Jarvis (1829–1913)

We do not believe that the heavens are sealed over our heads, but that the same Father who loved and cherished the children of Israel loves and cherishes us. We believe that we are as much in need of the assistance of our Heavenly Father in the directing of our lives as they were. We know that in the day and age in which we live the seal has been broken, and God has again spoken from the heavens.

—George Albert Smith (1870–1951)

[The Holy Ghost] satisfies and fills up every longing of the human heart, and fills up every vacuum. When I am filled with that Spirit, my soul is satisfied, and I can say in good earnest, that the trifling things of the day do not seem to stand in my way at all. But just let me lose my hold of that spirit and power of the Gospel, and partake of the spirit of the world, in the slightest degree, and trouble comes; there is something wrong. I am tried, and what will comfort me? You cannot impart comfort to me that will satisfy the immortal mind, but that which comes from the Fountain above. And is it not our privilege to so live that we can have this constantly flowing into our souls?

—Eliza R. Snow (1804–1877)

The greatest comfort in this life is the assurance of having a close relationship with God.

—David O. McKay (1873–1970)

If it were not for the assurance that I have that the Lord is near to us, guiding, directing, the burden would be almost beyond my strength, but I know that he is there, and that he can be appealed to, and if we have ears to hear attuned to him, we will never be left alone.

—Harold B. Lee (1899–1973)

Of what use is it that we know the truth, if we lack its spirit? Our knowledge, in this event, becomes a condemnation to us, failing to bear fruit. It is not sufficient that we know the truth, but we must be humble with this knowledge to possess the spirit to actuate us to good deeds. Baptism, as well as all other outward ordinances, without the spirit accompanying, is useless. We remain but baptized sinners.

—Joseph F. Smith (1838–1919)

The gift of the Holy Ghost. . . . quickens all the intellectual faculties, increases, enlarges, expands and purifies all the natural passions and affections; and adapts them, by the gift of wisdom, to their lawful use. It inspires, develops, cultivates and matures all the fine-toned sympathies, joys, tastes, kindred feelings and affections of our nature. It inspires virtue, kindness, goodness, tenderness, gentleness and charity. It develops beauty of person, form and features. It tends to health, vigor, animation and social feeling. It develops and invigorates all the faculties of the physical and intellectual man. It strengthens, invigorates, and gives tone to the nerves. In short, it is, as it were, marrow to the bone, joy to the heart, light to the eyes, music to the ears, and life to the whole being.

—Parley P. Pratt (1807–1857)

It is for us to do those things which the Lord requires at our hands, and leave the result with him.

—Brigham Young (1801–1877)

I would rather trust in the living God than in any other power on earth.

—John Taylor (1808–1887)

I will go forward. . . . I will smile at the rage of the tempest, and ride fearlessly and triumphantly across the boisterous ocean of circumstance. . . . And the testimony of Jesus will light up a lamp that will guide my vision through the portals of immortality, and communicate to my understanding the glories of the celestial kingdom.

—Eliza R. Snow (1804–1877)

What the world needs today more than anything else is an implicit faith in God, our Father, and in Jesus Christ, his Son, as the Redeemer of the world.

—Heber J. Grant (1856–1945)

Every noble impulse, every unselfish expression of love, every surrender of self to something higher than self, every loyalty to an ideal, every fine courage of the soul—by doing good for good's sake—that is spirituality.

—David O. McKay (1873–1970)

Whatever God requires is right, no matter what it is, although we may not see the reason thereof until all of the events transpire.

—Joseph Smith (1805–1844)

Patience is tied very closely to faith in our Heavenly Father. Actually, when we are unduly impatient, we are suggesting that we know what is best—better than does God. Or, at least, we are asserting that our timetable is better than his. Either way we are questioning the reality of God's omniscience, as if, as some seem to believe, God were on some sort of postdoctoral fellowship.

—Neal A. Maxwell (1926–2004)

We walked until our shoes were worn out, and our feet became sore and cracked open and bled until you could see the whole print of our feet with blood on the ground. We stopped and united in prayer to the Lord, we asked God the Eternal Father to heal our feet and our prayers were answered and our feet were healed forthwith.

—Jane Elizabeth Manning James (1822–1908)

Faith is not so much something we believe; faith is something we live.

—Joseph B. Wirthlin (1917–2008)

Without moral progress, stimulated by faith in God, immorality in all its forms will proliferate and strangle goodness and human decency. Mankind will not be able to fully express the potential nobility of the human soul unless faith in God is strengthened.

—James E. Faust (1920–2007)

Now, we will compare the word unto a seed. Now, if ye give place, that a seed may be planted in your heart, behold, if it be a true seed, or a good seed, if ye do not cast it out by your unbelief, that ye will resist the Spirit of the Lord, behold, it will begin to swell within your breasts; and when you feel these swelling motions, ye will begin to say within yourselves—It must needs be that this is a good seed, or that the word is good, for it beginneth to enlarge my soul; yea, it beginneth to enlighten my understanding, yea, it beginneth to be delicious to me.

—Book of Mormon, Alma 32:28

KNOWLEDGE
& EDUCATION

Mormons place much emphasis on the importance of education. Mormon boys and girls are admonished from an early age to seek out "the best books of wisdom" and to "seek learning even by study and also by faith" (Doctrine & Covenants 109:7). This admonition extends to both spiritual and secular learning.

Along with standard religious teachings such as honesty, chastity, and doing good to others, young Latter-day Saints are also strongly encouraged to get an education. The LDS Church has established several universities and colleges, as well as hundreds of seminaries, institutes, workforce and employment training centers, educational funds and charities, and schools to help achieve this goal.

Members of the LDS Church believe in an omniscient God who knows and understands all the laws and principles of science, mathematics, the arts, and all other disciplines (see **Creation**). Therefore, to grow in knowledge and wisdom is to become gradually more like him—one of the primary objectives of mortal existence (see **Divine Potential; Purpose of Life**).

—⁓—

The glory of God is intelligence, or, in other words, light and truth.

—Doctrine & Covenants 93:36

What is true education? It is awakening a love for truth; giving a just sense of duty; opening the eyes of the soul to the great purpose and end of life. It is not so much giving words, as thoughts; or mere maxims, as living principles. It is not teaching to be honest because "honesty is the best policy," but because it is right. It is teaching the individual to love the good, for the sake of the good; to be virtuous in action because one is so in heart; to love and serve God supremely, not from fear, but from delight in his perfect character.

—David O. McKay (1873–1970)

My culture idolizes the simplified woman, ardent and singular, bent to the collective and determined to serve it. The idea of the radiant mother, which I have been a part of for nearly forty years, is not something I would abandon. But a concomitant life beckoned, the life of those poets. It's one of the great human dilemmas: How could I live both lives and be fulfilled without sometimes neglecting one or the other? Mostly by being tired in the morning.

—Emma Lou Thayne (1924–2014)

No matter where we begin, if we pursue knowledge diligently and honestly our quest will inevitably lead us from the things of earth to the things of heaven.

—Hugh Nibley (1910–2005)

Knowing is a process, not an arrival.

—Emma Lou Thayne (1924–2014)

When, indeed, is a thing proven? Only when an individual has accumulated in his own consciousness enough observations, impressions, reasonings and feelings to satisfy him personally that it is so. The same evidence which convinces one expert may leave another completely unsatisfied.

—Hugh Nibley (1910–2005)

There will always be those little minds who, out of vanity or intellectual display, will attempt to destroy faith in the very foundations of life.

—Ezra Taft Benson (1899–1994)

A home without books or music—think of it—a house without furniture, a valley without rivers or babbling brooks; a forest without birds or sunshine!

—James A. Langton (1861–1943)

Someone has pointed out that books are among life's most precious possessions. They are the most remarkable creation of man. Nothing else that man builds ever lasts. Monuments fall, civilizations perish, but books continue. The perusal of a great book is as it were an interview with the noblest men of past ages who have written it.

—Sterling W. Sill (1903–1994)

It is the business of man to become acquainted with matter in all of its forms, so far as may be possible, in order to provide a foundation on which the reasoning mind of man may increasingly build its power.

—John A. Widtsoe (1872–1952)

There are some things you can give another person, and some things you cannot give him, except as he is willing to reach out and take them, and pay the price of making them a part of himself. This principle applies to studying, to developing talents, to absorbing knowledge, to acquiring skills, and to the learning of all the lessons of life.

—Richard L. Evans (1906–1971)

Whatever principle of intelligence we attain unto in this life, it will rise with us in the resurrection. And if a person gains more knowledge and intelligence in this life through his diligence and obedience than another, he will have so much the advantage in the world to come.

—Doctrine & Covenants 130:18–19

We should never assume that because something is unexplainable *by us*, that it is unexplainable.

—Neal A. Maxwell (1926–2004)

One cannot know God nor understand his works or plans unless he follows the laws which govern. The spiritual realm, which is just as absolute as is the physical, cannot be understood by the laws of the physical. You do not learn to make electric generators in a seminary. Neither do you learn certain truths about spiritual things in a physics laboratory. You must go to the spiritual laboratory, use the facilities available there, and comply with the governing rules. Then you may know of these truths just as surely, or more surely, than the scientist knows the metals, or the acids, or other elements.

—Spencer W. Kimball (1895–1985)

In an infinite universe, one cannot possibly learn all or do all, at once. A beginning must be made somewhere and corner by corner, department by department, space by space, all will be known and conquered. In the end, all must be explored, and whether one begins in the east or the west cannot matter much. The big concern is the extent to which a man offers himself, mind and body, to his worthwhile work. Upon that will growth depend.

—John A. Widtsoe (1872–1952)

Of all treasures of knowledge, the most vital is the knowledge of God, his existence, powers, love, and promises.

—Spencer W. Kimball (1895–1985)

That motherhood brings into a woman's life a richness, zest, and tone that nothing else ever can I gladly grant you, but that her usefulness ends there, or that she has no other individual interests to serve I cannot so readily concede.
—Emmeline B. Wells (1828–1921)

Education is the power to think clearly, the power to act well in the world's work, and the power to appreciate life.
—Brigham Young (1801–1877)

All scholarship, like all science, is an ongoing, open-ended discussion in which all conclusions are tentative forever, the principal value and charm of the game being the discovery of the totally unexpected.
—Hugh Nibley (1910–2005)

I do not care how learned a man may be, or how extensively he may have traveled; I do not care what his talent, intellect or genius may be, at what college he may have studied, how comprehensive his views or what his judgment may be on other matters, he cannot understand certain things without the Spirit of God, and that necessarily introduces the principle . . . of revelation.

—John Taylor (1808–1887)

You are sent to this world with a very serious purpose. You are sent to school, for that matter, to begin as a human infant and grow to unbelievable proportions in wisdom, judgment, knowledge, and power.

—Spencer W. Kimball (1895–1985)

It is a paradox that men will gladly devote time every day for many years to learn a science or an art; yet will expect to win a knowledge of the gospel, which comprehends all sciences and arts, through perfunctory glances at books or occasional listening to sermons. The gospel should be studied more intensively than any school or college subject. They who pass opinion on the gospel without having given it intimate and careful study are not lovers of truth, and their opinions are worthless. To secure a testimony, then, study must accompany desire and prayer.

—John A. Widtsoe (1872–1952)

Doctors and trainers often see perfectly developed bodies, but nobody can even begin to imagine what a perfect *mind* would be like; that is where the whole range of progress and growth must take place.

—Hugh Nibley (1910–2005)

Do not be discouraged because you cannot learn all at once; learn one thing at a time, learn it well, and treasure it up, then learn another truth and treasure that up, and in a few years you will have a great store of useful knowledge.
　　　　—Wilford Woodruff (1807–1898)

There are some who do not learn, and who do not improve as fast as they might, because their eyes and their hearts are not upon God; they do not reflect neither do they have that knowledge which they might have; they miss a good deal which they might receive. We have got to obtain knowledge before we obtain permanent happiness; we have got to be wide awake in the things of God.
　　　　—Lorenzo Snow (1814–1901)

Pure intelligence comprises not only knowledge, but also the power to properly apply that knowledge.
　　　　—Joseph F. Smith (1838–1919)

Knowledge can be heady stuff, but it easily leads to an excess of zeal!—to illusions of grandeur and a desire to impress others and achieve eminence. . . . Our search for knowledge should be ceaseless, which means that it is open-ended, never resting on laurels, degrees, or past achievements.

—Hugh Nibley (1910–2005)

I've always had an inquiring mind. I'm not satisfied just to accept things. I like to follow through and study things out. I learned early to put aside those gospel questions that I couldn't answer. I had a shelf of things I didn't understand, but as I've grown older and studied and prayed and thought about each problem, one by one I've been able to better understand them. . . . I still have some questions on that shelf, but I've come to understand so many other things in my life that I'm willing to bide my time for the rest of the answers.

—Camilla Eyring Kimball (1894–1987)

True education does not consist merely in the acquiring of a few facts of science, history, literature or art, but in the development of character.

—David O. McKay (1873–1970)

We are in a great school, and we should be diligent to learn, and continue to store up the knowledge of heaven and of earth, and read good books, although I cannot say that I would recommend the reading of all books, for it is not all books which are good. Read good books, and extract from them wisdom and understanding as much as you possibly can, aided by the Spirit of God.

—Brigham Young (1801–1877)

We believe in all truth, no matter to what subject it may refer. No sect or religious denomination—or, I may say, no searcher of truth—in the world possesses a single principle of truth that we do not accept or that we will reject. We are willing to receive all truth, from whatever source it may come; for truth will stand, truth will endure.

—Joseph F. Smith (1838–1919)

Things that appear unlikely, impossible, or paradoxical from one point of view often make perfectly good sense from another.

—Hugh Nibley (1910–2005)

A man may possess a profound knowledge of history and mathematics; he may be an authority in psychology, biology, or astronomy; he may know all the discovered truths pertaining to geology and natural science; but if he has not with this knowledge that nobility of soul which prompts him to deal justly with his fellow men, to practice virtue and holiness in his personal life, he is not truly an educated man.

—David O. McKay (1873–1970)

It is the mark of a truly educated man to know what not to read.

—Ezra Taft Benson (1899–1994)

The mere stuffing of the mind with a knowledge of facts is not education. The mind must not only possess a knowledge of the truth, but the soul must revere it, cherish it, love it as a priceless gem; and this human life must be guided and shaped by it in order to fulfill its destiny.

—Joseph Fielding Smith (1876–1972)

If men are really humble, they will realize that they discover, but do not create, truth.

—Spencer W. Kimball (1895–1985)

The education of the mind and the education of the body should go hand in hand. A skillful brain should be joined with a skillful hand. Manual labor should be dignified among us and always be made honorable. . . . Every one should make it a matter of pride to be a producer, and not a consumer alone. Our children should be taught to sustain themselves by their own industry and skill, and not only do this, but to help sustain others, and that to do this by honest toil is one of the most honorable means which God has furnished to his children here on earth.

—Wilford Woodruff (1807–1898)

It matters little whether one is a plumber, or a banker, or a farmer, for these occupations are secondary; what is most important is what one knows and believes concerning his past and his future and what he does about it.

—Spencer W. Kimball (1895–1985)

The gas-law of learning: . . . any amount of information no matter how small will fill any intellectual void no matter how large.

—Hugh Nibley (1910–2005)

Any intelligent man may learn what he wants to learn. He may acquire knowledge in any field, though it requires much thought and effort. It takes more than a decade to get a high school diploma; it takes an additional four years for most people to get a college degree; it takes nearly a quarter-century to become a great physician. Why, oh why do people think they can fathom the most complex spiritual depths without the necessary experimental and laboratory work accompanied by compliance with the laws that govern it?

—Spencer W. Kimball (1895–1985)

There is no knowledge, no light, no wisdom that you are in possession of, but what you have received it from some source.

—Brigham Young (1801–1877)

We saw our father and mother read, and they read to us. It did something of an indefinable nature. It gave us a familiarity with good books. We felt at home and at ease with them. They were not strangers to us. They were as friends, willing to give to us if we were willing to make a little effort.

—Gordon B. Hinckley (1910–2008)

As knowledge increases, the verdict of yesterday must be reversed today, and in the long run the most positive authority is the least to be trusted.

—Hugh Nibley (1910–2005)

Seek ye diligently and teach one another words of wisdom; yea, seek ye out of the best books words of wisdom, seek learning even by study and also by faith.

—Doctrine & Covenants 109:7

HOME & FAMILY

Mormons believe that families can be together forever, not just till death. The family is the single most important unit of society. The home can be the most sacred of settings on Earth, surpassing even that of the Church's holy temples. This is perhaps because the home is where parents can have the greatest positive influence upon their children, teach them the principles of the happiness, and encourage and support them in their pursuit of worthwhile goals.

In addition to regularly attending Church services and activities, Latter-day Saint families are admonished to gather together once a week—typically Monday evenings—for what's called family home evening. This weekly family gathering commonly involves a spiritual lesson and a wholesome, fun activity—and, hopefully, something sweet and delicious to enjoy. Family home evening helps teach children correct principles and strengthen family bonds through mutual appreciation, love, and respect.

For Mormons, peace, unity, and harmony in the home are considered to be of utmost importance.

—⚉—

The divine plan of happiness enables family relationships to be perpetuated beyond the grave. Sacred ordinances and covenants available in holy temples make it possible for individuals to return to the presence of God and for families to be united eternally.

—*The Family: A Proclamation to the World* (1995)

All the comfort I can take in this or any other life will be in the company of all my children and grandchildren.

—Mary Minerva Dart Judd (1838–1909)

There can be no genuine happiness separate and apart from the home, and every effort made to sanctify and preserve its influence is uplifting to those who toil and sacrifice for its establishment. . . . There is no happiness without service, and there is no greater service than that which converts the home into a divine institution, and which promotes and preserves family life.

—Joseph F. Smith (1838–1919)

Live in such a way, in love and kindness, that peace and prayer and thanksgiving will be in your homes together. Do not let your homes just be a place to hang your hats at night and get your meals and then run off some place else but let your homes be the abiding place of the Spirit of the Lord.

—George Albert Smith (1870–1951)

Family home evening is . . . for the purpose of teaching values and gospel principles, displaying talents, and enjoying different kinds of family fun and activities.

—Stephen R. Covey (1932–2012)

Historically, the family has played the primary role in educating children for life, with the school providing supplemental scaffolding to the family.

—Stephen R. Covey (1932–2012)

We have a wonderful Church organization, but the one place where we may have greater influence than any other is in the homes in which we reside. We have our Sabbath schools, our Mutual Improvement Associations, our Relief Societies, our Primaries, our Church schools and seminaries. All these institutions are intended to develop the best that is in mankind, but we as parents of children in this Church have no right to place the responsibility upon these organizations to establish faith in the hearts of these children that God has placed in our homes. It is your duty and mine to teach the children that come to our homes.

—George Albert Smith (1870–1951)

Let my assure you, Brethren, that some day you will have a personal priesthood interview with the Savior, himself. If you are interested, I will tell you the order in which he will ask you to account for your earthly responsibilities.

First, he will request an accountability report about your relationship with your wife. Have you actively been engaged in making her happy and ensuring that her needs have been met as an individual?

Second, he will want an accountability report about each of your children individually. He will not attempt to have this for simply a family stewardship but will request information about your relationship to each and every child.

—David O. McKay (1873–1970)

The most important of the Lord's work you will ever do will be the work you do within the walls of your own home.

—Harold B. Lee (1899–1973)

When it comes to developing character strength, inner security, and unique personal and interpersonal talents and skills in a child, no institution can or ever will compare with, or effectively substitute for, the home's potential for positive influence.

—Stephen R. Covey (1932–2012)

Oh, brothers and sisters, families can be forever! Do not let the lures of the moment draw you away from them! Divinity, eternity, and family—they go together, hand in hand, and so must we!

—Spencer W. Kimball (1895–1985)

Our parents deserve our honor and respect for giving us life itself. Beyond this they almost always made countless sacrifices as they cared for and nurtured us through our infancy and childhood, provided us with the necessities of life, and nursed us through physical illnesses and the emotional stresses of growing up.

—Ezra Taft Benson (1899–1994)

If I were to think, as so many think, that now that my beloved wife and my beloved parents are gone, that they have passed out of my life forever and that I shall never see them again, it would deprive me of one of the greatest joys that I have in life: the contemplation of meeting them again, and receiving their welcome and their affection.

—George Albert Smith (1870–1951)

Build traditions of family vacations and trips and outings. These memories will never be forgotten by your children.

—Ezra Taft Benson (1899–1994)

A worried society now begins to see that the disintegration of the family brings upon the world the calamities foretold by the prophets. The world's councils and deliberations will succeed only when they define the family as the Lord has revealed it to be. "Except the Lord build the house, they labour in vain that build it" (Ps. 127:1).

—Howard W. Hunter (1907–1995)

Salvation is a family affair.

—Bruce R. McConkie (1915–1985)

The average family spends thirty hours [a week] in front of a television, and they say they don't have the time to have a balanced, integrated life.

—Stephen R. Covey (1932–2012)

I know of no other place than home where more happiness can be found in this life. It is possible to make home a bit of heaven; indeed, I picture heaven to be a continuation of the ideal home.

—David O. McKay (1873–1970)

We warn that individuals who violate covenants of chastity, who abuse spouse or offspring, or who fail to fulfill family responsibilities will one day stand accountable before God. Further, we warn that the disintegration of the family will bring upon individuals, communities, and nations the calamities foretold by ancient and modern prophets.

—*The Family: A Proclamation to the World* (1995)

RECREATION

Religion in general is often associated with sober seriousness and not having fun. Certainly there are teachings about the kinds of recreation that Mormons are and aren't supposed to participate in. For example, Mormons strive to avoid pornography in any form.

At the same time, LDS leaders since the time of Joseph Smith have taught the importance of wholesome recreation. Confronted by visitors who were surprised to see a prophet playing ball, Joseph Smith is said to have compared his sports participation to a hunter unstringing his bow so it doesn't lose its elasticity. "The prophet said it was just so with his mind, he did not want it strung up all the time," one visitor reported.

In this same spirit, Mormons today participate in hard work, spiritual devotion, and service to others—but also in organized recreational activities, individual hobbies, and entertainment. All of these are seen as part of living a balanced life.

—◁◈▷—

Successful marriages and families are established and maintained on principles of faith, prayer, repentance, forgiveness, respect, love, compassion, work, and wholesome recreational activities.

—*The Family: A Proclamation to the World* (1995)

Wholesome recreation is part of our religion, and a change of pace is necessary, and even its anticipation can lift the spirit.

—Ezra Taft Benson (1899–1994)

I had not a chance to dance . . . and never heard the enchanting tones of the violin, until I was eleven years of age; and then I thought I was on the highway to hell, if I suffered myself to linger and listen to it. I shall not subject my little children to such a course of unnatural training, but they shall go to the dance, study music, read novels, and do anything else that will tend to expand their frames, add fire to their spirits, improve their minds, and make them feel free, and untrammeled in body and mind.

—Brigham Young (1801–1877)

Amusements people will have. It is needful and right that these should be provided.

—Joseph F. Smith (1838–1919)

There is no enjoyment, no comfort, no pleasure, nothing that the human heart can imagine, with all the spirit of revelation we can get, that tends to beautify, happify, make comfortable and peaceful, and exalt the feelings of mortals, but what the Lord has in store for his people. He never objected to their taking comfort.
—Brigham Young (1801–1877)

With the great message the Latter-day Saints have to bear, should we be putting on plays? The answer is decidedly, yes. Narrowing individual or community life too much is not wholesome.
—Joseph J. Cannon (1877–1945)

The ideals and daily lives of a people are judged by their standards of amusements.
—Levi Edgar Young (1874–1963)

Amusement is not the purpose of life; it should be indulged in only by way of variety. When people accustom themselves to constant or oft-repeated rounds of pleasure, the true objects of human existence are forgotten and duty becomes irksome and detestable.

—Joseph F. Smith (1838–1919)

I believe that it is necessary for the Saints to have amusement, but it must be of the proper kind. I do not believe the Lord intends and desires that we should pull a long face and look sanctimonious and hypocritical. I think he expects us to be happy and of a cheerful countenance, but he does not expect of us the indulgence in boisterous and unseemly conduct and the seeking after the vain and foolish things which amuse and entertain the world. He has commanded us to the contrary for our own good and eternal welfare.

—Joseph Fielding Smith (1876–1972)

It is the privilege of the Saints to enjoy every good thing, for the earth and its fulness belong to the Lord, and he has promised all to his faithful Saints; but it must be enjoyed without spirit of covetousness and selfishness—without the spirit of lust, and in the spirit of the Gospel; then the sun will shine sweetly upon us; each day will be filled with delight, and all things will be filled with beauty, giving joy, pleasure, and rest to the Saints.

—Brigham Young (1801–1877)

MARRIAGE

Traditionally in the Christian world, marriages are performed "till death do you part." Mormon marriages, on the other hand, are designed to last forever.

Latter-day Saints refer to marriage ceremonies performed in LDS temples as "sealings," alluding to similar language used in the New Testament: "whatsoever thou shalt bind on earth shall be bound in heaven" (Matthew 16:19). These sealings are intended to bind couples—husband to wife, wife to husband—for all eternity.

Mormons generally reject the notion of soul mates, as well as the idea that one must find the "right" person to marry. Instead, Latter-day

Saints seeking marriage are instructed to first become someone worth marrying. Almost any couple that is willing to work for it can enjoy a happy and successful marriage. Except for extreme circumstances, divorce is generally discouraged. Mormons are also taught that marriage is an equal partnership, with husbands and wives praying and counseling with one another over important family decisions. Married couples are to love, respect, honor, and remain faithful to one another throughout life.

The LDS Church has received strong criticism in recent history due to its support of marriage as a purely heterosexual union. Though many Mormons do politically support homosexual civil unions and other gay rights, they generally view marriage as a divinely ordained institution and, as such, one over which God has the ultimate authority.

—᚜—

Marriage between man and woman is essential to his eternal plan. Children are entitled to birth within the bonds of matrimony, and to be reared by a father and a mother who honor marital vows with complete fidelity. Happiness in family life is most likely to be achieved when founded upon the teachings of the Lord Jesus Christ.

—*The Family: A Proclamation to the World* (1995)

You should express regularly to your wife and children your reverence and respect for her. Indeed, one of the greatest things a father can do for his children is to love their mother.

—Howard W. Hunter (1907–1995)

Unless you and your mate are united in purpose, dedication, and loyalty, you will not succeed to the extent you otherwise could.

—Ezra Taft Benson (1899–1994)

Being happily and successfully married is generally not so much a matter of marrying the right person as it is being the right person.

—Howard W. Hunter (1907–1995)

Marriage is the preserver of the human race. Without it, the purposes of God would be frustrated; virtue would be destroyed to give place to vice and corruption, and the earth would be void and empty.

—Joseph F. Smith (1838–1919)

Let husband and wife never speak to one another in loud tones, unless the house is on fire.

—David O. McKay (1873–1970)

If a young man or a young woman has no opportunity of getting married, and they live faithful lives up to the time of their death, they will have all the blessings, exaltation, and glory that any man or woman will have who had this opportunity and improved it.

—Lorenzo Snow (1814–1901)

My mother once said that if you meet a girl in whose presence you feel a desire to achieve, who inspires you to do your best, and to make the most of yourself, such a young woman is worthy of your love and is awakening love in your heart.

—George Q. Morris (1874–1962)

How sweet is the assurance, how comforting is the peace that come from the knowledge that if we marry right and live right, our relationship will continue, notwithstanding the certainty of death and the passage of time. Men may write love songs and sing them. They may yearn and hope and dream. But all of this will be only a romantic longing unless there is an exercise of authority that transcends the powers of time and death.

—Gordon B. Hinckley (1910–2008)

The place of woman in the Church is to walk beside the man, not in front of him nor behind him. In the Church there is full equality between man and woman. The gospel, which is the only concern of the Church, was devised by the Lord for men and women alike

—John A. Widtsoe (1872–1952)

Marriage is a partnership. Someone has observed that in the Bible account of the creation woman was not formed from a part of man's head, suggesting that she might rule over him, nor from a part of a man's foot that she was to be trampled under his feet. Woman was taken from man's side as though to emphasize the fact that she was always to be by his side as a partner and companion.

—Harold B. Lee (1899–1973)

Soul mates are fiction and an illusion; and while every young man and young woman will seek with all diligence and prayerfulness to find a mate with whom life can be most compatible and beautiful, yet it is certain that almost any good man and any good woman can have happiness and a successful marriage if both are willing to pay the price.

—Spencer W. Kimball (1895–1985)

The first commandment that God gave to Adam and Eve pertained to their potential for parenthood as husband and wife. . . . God has commanded that the sacred powers of procreation are to be employed only between man and woman, lawfully wedded as husband and wife. We declare the means by which mortal life is created to be divinely appointed. We affirm the sanctity of life and of its importance in God's eternal plan.

—*The Family: A Proclamation to the World* (1995)

Many couples permit their marriages to become stale and their love to grow cold like old bread or worn-out jokes or cold gravy. These people will do well to reevaluate, to renew their courting, to express their affection, to acknowledge kindness, and to increase their consideration so their marriage again can become beautiful, sweet, and growing. While marriage is difficult, and discordant and frustrated marriages are common, yet real, lasting happiness is possible, and marriage can be more an exultant ecstasy than the human mind can conceive.

—Spencer W. Kimball (1895–1985)

What does it mean to love someone with all your heart? It means to love with all your emotional feelings and with all your devotion. Surely when you love your wife with all your heart, you cannot demean her, criticize her, find fault with her, or abuse her by words, sullen behavior, or actions.

—Ezra Taft Benson (1899–1994)

To their joint enterprise of marriage, Father and Mother brought diversity; to each other, they brought each other; and to us, they brought a happy journey into adulthood. If there was a "head" of our home, I couldn't define it. . . . Whatever one did—in work, play, church, or civic activities—the other participated in vicariously. Theirs was not a dependency, not a leaning, but a sharing and receiving of support. They took genuine delight in each other's triumphs and lent constant understanding to each other's concerns, hurts, and failures.

—Emma Lou Thayne (1924–2014)

Husbands, recognize your wife's intelligence and her ability to counsel with you as a real partner regarding family plans, family activities, and family budgeting. Don't be stingy with your time or with your means. Give her the opportunity to grow intellectually, emotionally, and socially as well as spiritually.

—Ezra Taft Benson (1899–1994)

True love is not so much a matter of romance as it is a matter of anxious concern for the well-being of one's companion.

—Gordon B. Hinckley (1910–2008)

Marriage, in its truest sense, is a partnership of equals, with neither exercising dominion over the other, but, rather, with each encouraging and assisting the other in whatever responsibilities and aspirations he or she might have.

—Gordon B. Hinckley (1910–2008)

As we got closer to marriage, I felt completely confident that Gordon loved me. But I also knew somehow that I would never come first with him. I knew I was going to be second in his life and that the Lord was going to be first. And that was okay. It seemed to me that if you understood the gospel and the purpose of our being here, you would want a husband who put the Lord first.

—Marjorie Pay Hinckley (1911–2004)

One good yardstick as to whether a person might be the right one for you is this: in her presence, do you think your noblest thoughts, do you aspire to your finest deeds, do you wish you were better than you are?

—Ezra Taft Benson (1899–1994)

My big, athletic father was afraid of rattlesnakes. My mother would go out there, armed with that shovel. We'd call Mother and she'd take care of whatever needed to be taken care of. It was a metaphor for the way they lived. They both operated from strength, not from weakness, and they brought a kind of wholeness to each other.

—Emma Lou Thayne (1924–2014)

We make no greater voluntary choice in this life than the selection of a marriage partner. This decision can bring eternal happiness and joy. To find sublime fulfillment in marriage, both partners need to be fully committed to the marriage.

—James E. Faust (1920–2007)

Don't let this choice [of a marriage partner] ever be made except with earnest, searching, prayerful consideration, confiding in parents [and] in faithful, mature, trustworthy friends.

—Richard L. Evans (1906–1971)

The remedy for most marital stress is not in divorce. It is in repentance and forgiveness, in sincere expressions of charity and service. It is not in separation. It is in simple integrity that leads a man and a woman to square up their shoulders and meet their obligations. It is found in the Golden Rule, a time-honored principle that should first and foremost find expression in marriage.

—Gordon B. Hinckley (1910–2008)

PARENTING

Raising children is sometimes called the hardest and most important job in the world. Mormons largely agree. In the Mormon view, perhaps no other experience in this world brings us a greater understanding of God's nature than parenting (see **Heavenly Parents; Divine Potential**).

As children of a loving Heavenly Father, Latter-day Saints see their duty to raise and protect their own children in love and righteousness as training to become more like him (see **Purpose of Life**). This responsibility takes priority over other areas of life, including professional advancement, hobbies, involvement in social causes, and even service in the Church.

Few other aspects of day-to-day living receive more emphasis in Church talks, lessons, and conversations than how to be a successful parent.

—⁓—

Parents have a sacred duty to rear their children in love and righteousness, to provide for their physical and spiritual needs, and to teach them to love and serve one another, observe the commandments of God, and be law-abiding citizens wherever they live. Husbands and wives—mothers and fathers—will be held accountable before God for the discharge of these obligations.

—*The Family: A Proclamation to the World* (1995)

We should never permit ourselves to do anything that we are not willing to see our children do.

—Brigham Young (1801–1877)

It is true intelligence for a man to take a subject that is mysterious and great in itself and to unfold and simplify it so that a child can understand it.

—John Taylor (1808–1887)

The importance of the mother in building a secure, loving, stimulating environment in which children can grow up as healthy and self-reliant individuals is very important. . . . But not all situations are ideal. Not all women are mothers, and not all mothers have children at home. Furthermore, not all mothers can make the choice to be home with their children all of the time. Often circumstances constrain their choices. At other times, other responsibilities and opportunities require that difficult decisions be made. Women and families will be happier with these decisions if they are made using both study and faith.
—Chieko N. Okazaki (1926–2011)

To be a successful father or a successful mother is greater than to be a successful general or a successful statesman. One is universal and eternal greatness, the other is ephemeral.
—Joseph F. Smith (1838–1919)

Anyone who would say apologetically, "I am only a homemaker," has not fully appreciated the importance and intricacy of her profession. Some of the attributes required to be a successful mother are an unlimited amount of love, patience, unselfishness, and endurance. A mother should be skilled in child training, in economics and management, in nutrition and nursing; in fact, a well-rounded education will be a great help in her important role both as wife and mother.

—Camilla Eyring Kimball (1894–1987)

If you can only convince your children that you love them, that your soul goes out to them for their good, that you are their truest friend, they, in turn, will place confidence in you and will love you and seek to do your bidding.

—Joseph F. Smith (1838–1919)

In the home in which there is an intelligent and spiritually strong mother dwells the greatest single influence on the spiritual and moral strength of the family nurtured there.

—Camilla Eyring Kimball (1894–1987)

A mother that is successful in raising a good boy, or girl, to imitate her example and to follow her precepts through life, sows the seeds of virtue, honor, and integrity and of righteousness in their hearts that will be felt through all their career in life; and wherever that boy or girl goes, as man or woman, in whatever society they mingle, the good effects of the example of that mother upon them will be felt; and it will never die, because it will extend from them to their children from generation to generation.

—Joseph F. Smith (1838–1919)

Motherhood is the greatest potential influence either for good or ill in human life. The mother's image is the first that stamps itself on the unwritten page of the young child's mind. It is her caress that first awakens a sense of security; her kiss, the first realization of affection; her sympathy and tenderness, the first assurance that there is love in the world.

—David O. McKay (1873–1970)

By divine design, fathers are to preside over their families in love and righteousness and are responsible to provide the necessities of life and protection for their families. Mothers are primarily responsible for the nurture of their children. In these sacred responsibilities, fathers and mothers are obligated to help one another as equal partners.

—*The Family: A Proclamation to the World* (1995)

The gospel gives to Latter-day Saint mothers the loftiest concept of home and family life known to mankind.

—Belle S. Spafford (1895–1982)

Children are more influenced by sermons you act than by sermons you preach.

—David O. McKay (1873–1970)

Those things which we call extraordinary, remarkable, or unusual may make history, but they do not make real life. After all, to do well those things which God ordained to be the common lot of all mankind, is the truest greatness. To be a successful father or a successful mother is greater than to be a successful general or a successful statesman.

—Joseph F. Smith (1838–1919)

Of course we believe in children. The Lord has told us to multiply and replenish the earth that we might have joy in our posterity, and there is no greater joy than the joy that comes of happy children in good families. But he did not designate the number, nor has the Church. That is a sacred matter left to the couple and the Lord.
—Gordon B. Hinckley (1910–2008)

Parents must try to be, or at least put forth their best efforts to be, what they wish the children to be. It is impossible for you to be an example of what you are not.
—Joseph Fielding Smith (1876–1972)

No matter what you read or hear, no matter what the difference of circumstances you observe in the lives of women about you, it is important for you Latter-day Saint women to understand that the Lord holds motherhood and mothers sacred and in the highest esteem. He has entrusted to his daughters the great responsibility of bearing and nurturing children . . . . There is divinity in each new life.

—Spencer W. Kimball (1895–1985)

A righteous father protects his children with his time and presence.

—Howard W. Hunter (1907–1995)

Anybody who thinks that being a wife and mother is a dull occupation doesn't take the daily challenges seriously. The family is the biggest field for learning there is. That's where you need to work double time to learn all you can. There's no end for the need to study.

—Camilla Eyring Kimball (1894–1987)

Parents have no greater responsibility in this world than the bringing up of their children in the right way, and they will have no greater satisfaction as the years pass than to see those children grow in integrity and honesty and make something of their lives.

—Gordon B. Hinckley (1910–2008)

My parents were just constantly affirming me in everything that I did. Late at night, I'd wake up and hear my mother talking over my bed, saying, "You're going to do great on this test. You can do anything you want."

—Stephen R. Covey (1932–2012)

Children will not remember you for the material things you provided but for the feeling that you cherished them.

—Richard L. Evans (1906–1971)

When the real history of mankind is fully disclosed, will it feature the echoes of gunfire or the shaping sound of lullabies? The great armistices made by military men or the peacemaking of women in homes and in neighborhoods? Will what happened in cradles and kitchens prove to be more controlling than what happened in congresses?

—Neal A. Maxwell (1926–2004)

To be a good father and mother requires that the parents defer many of their own needs and desires in favor of the needs of their children. As a consequence of this sacrifice, conscientious parents develop a nobility of character and learn to put into practice the selfless truths taught by the Savior himself.

—James E. Faust (1920–2007)

CHOICES & FREEDOM

Dystopian novels and films (particularly those aimed at a young-adult audience) have experienced a remarkable surge in popularity in recent years. Nearly all these stories share one common theme: the struggle for individual rights and freedom against authoritarian control. Mormonism highlights a similar theme: "Satan rebelled against me, and sought to destroy the agency of man, which I, the Lord God, had given him" (Moses 4:3).

For Mormons, the freedom to make one's own choices is considered one of the greatest gifts (if not *the* greatest gift) that God has given us. This gift was integral to the plan of salvation that God presented his children during premortal life (see **Heavenly Parents; Divine Potential**). Without this freedom, we could not exercise faith, gain experience, or become more like him (see **Purpose of Life** and **Trials**).

In Mormon theology, it's understood that freedom of choice is meaningless without opposition in all things. The gift of free agency was so precious that it must allow for mankind to be tempted: "Wherefore, the Lord God gave unto man that he should act for himself. Wherefore, man could not act for himself save it should be that he was enticed by the one or the other" (2 Nephi 2:16).

Mormons are encouraged and encourage others to use their free will wisely (see **Priorities**).

—⁂—

God has given to all men an agency and has granted to us the privilege to serve him or serve him not, to do that which is right or that which is wrong, and this privilege is given to all men irrespective of creed, color, or condition. The wealthy have this agency, the poor have this agency, and no man is deprived by any power of God from exercising it in the fullest and in the freest manner. This agency has been given to all. This is a blessing that God has bestowed upon the world of mankind, upon all his children alike.

—Joseph F. Smith (1838–1919)

God gave his children their free agency even in the spirit world, by which the individual spirits had the privilege, just as men have here, of choosing the good and rejecting the evil, or partaking of the evil to suffer the consequences of their sins.

—Joseph Fielding Smith (1876–1972)

Freedom of choice is more to be treasured than any possession earth can give.
—David O. McKay (1873–1970)

I am more afraid that this people have so much confidence in their leaders that they will not inquire for themselves of God whether they are led by him. I am fearful they will settle down in a state of blind self-security. Let every man and woman know, by the whispering of the Spirit of God to themselves, whether their leaders are walking in the path the Lord dictates, or not.
—Brigham Young (1801–1877)

Every human has four endowments—self-awareness, conscience, independent will, and creative imagination. These give us the ultimate human freedom. . . . The power to choose, to respond, to change.
—Stephen R. Covey (1932–2012)

Each individual is entitled to determine the ultimate destiny of his or her life. We can choose to use the powers within to have a happy life of continual growth and development that leads to eternal progression, or we can choose to follow the crowd of other people struggling to a top that leads to nowhere.

—Barbara B. Smith (1922–2010)

As precious as life itself is our heritage of individual freedom, for man's free agency is a God-given gift.

—David O. McKay (1873–1970)

Life gives to all the choice. You can satisfy yourself with mediocrity if you wish. You can be common, ordinary, dull, colorless, or you can channel your life so that it will be clean, vibrant, useful, progressive, colorful, and rich.

—Spencer W. Kimball (1895–1985)

We are free to choose, but we are not free to alter the consequences of those choices.
—Ezra Taft Benson (1899–1994)

Don't be like anybody else. Be different. Then you can make a contribution. Otherwise, you just echo something; you're just a reflection.
—Hugh Nibley (1910–2005)

It is not meet that I should command in all things; for he that is compelled in all things, the same is a slothful and not a wise servant; wherefore he receiveth no reward.

Verily I say, men should be anxiously engaged in a good cause, and do many things of their own free will, and bring to pass much righteousness;

For the power is in them, wherein they are agents unto themselves. And inasmuch as men do good they shall in nowise lose their reward.
—Doctrine & Covenants 58:26-28

Opposition to God and his Christ, opposition to light and truth has existed since the beginning to the present day. This is the warfare that commenced in heaven, that has existed through all time, and that will continue until the winding up scene, until he reigns whose right it is to reign, when he shall come in clouds of glory to reward every man according to the deeds done in the body.

—Wilford Woodruff (1807–1898)

Wherefore, men are free according to the flesh; and all things are given them which are expedient unto man. And they are free to choose liberty and eternal life, through the great Mediator of all men, or to choose captivity and death, according to the captivity and power of the devil; for he seeketh that all men might be miserable like unto himself.

—Book of Mormon, 2 Nephi 2:27

My most earnest prayer is that every man and every woman will get it into his or her heart that they are in very deed the architects of their lives.

—Heber J. Grant (1856–1945)

And it must needs be that the devil should tempt the children of men, or they could not be agents unto themselves; for if they never should have bitter they could not know the sweet.

—Doctrine & Covenants 29:39

Wherefore, because that Satan rebelled against me, and sought to destroy the agency of man, which I, the Lord God, had given him, and also, that I should give unto him mine own power; by the power of mine Only Begotten, I caused that he should be cast down.

—Pearl of Great Price, Moses 4:3

All good things require effort. That which is worth having will cost part of your physical being, your intellectual power and your soul power. Let us ever keep in mind that life is largely what we make it.

    —David O. McKay (1873–1970)

God's chief way of acting is by persuasion and patience and long-suffering, not by coercion and stark confrontation. He acts by gentle solicitation and by sweet enticement. He always acts with unfailing respect for the freedom and independence that we possess.

    —Howard W. Hunter (1907–1995)

PRIORITIES

Hand-in-hand with the freedom to choose is the need to make wise choices among the many options life offers (see **Choices & Freedom**). These decisions include choices in how we will use our energy, material resources, spiritual and intellectual focus, and, perhaps most importantly, our time.

In the Mormon view, life on Earth is all about opportunities (see **Purpose of Life**). We literally choose what it is that we will become. Such decisions are often about choosing among competing good activities, as well as choosing between right and wrong.

—⁂—

Where the Lord plants us, there we are to stand; when he requires us to exert ourselves for the support of these holy principles, that we are to do; that is all we need to trouble ourselves about; the rest our Heavenly Father will take care of.

—Lorenzo Snow (1814–1901)

I would rather be a doorkeeper in the House of the Lord than mingle with the top brass in the tents of the wicked.

—Hugh Nibley (1910–2005)

The god of the world is the gold and the silver. The world worships this god. It is all-powerful to them, though they might not be willing to acknowledge it. Now, it is designed, in the providence of God, that the Latter-day Saints should show whether they have so far advanced in the knowledge, in the wisdom, and in the power of God that they cannot be overcome by the god of the world. We must come to that point. We have also got to reach another standard, a higher plane: we have got to love God more than we love the world, more than we love gold or silver, and love our neighbor as ourselves.

—Lorenzo Snow (1814–1901)

Wealth is a jealous master who will not be served halfheartedly and will suffer no rival—not even God: "Ye cannot serve God and Mammon" (Matthew 6:24). In return for unquestioning obedience, wealth promises security, power, position, and honors—in fact, anything in this world. . . . The more important wealth is, the less important it is how one gets it.

—Hugh Nibley (1910–2005)

If we choose the right, success will be ours, and the achievement of it will have molded and formed and created us into the kind of person qualified to be accepted into the presence of God.

—Harold B. Lee (1899–1973)

Any task in life is easier if we approach it with the one-at-a-time attitude. . . . To cite a whimsical saying: "If you chase two rabbits, both of them will escape." No one is adequate to do everything all at once. We have to select what is important, what is possible, and begin where we are, with what we have. And if we begin and if we keep going the weight, the worry, the doubt, the depression will begin to lift. . . . "The beginning," said Plato, "is the most important part."

—Richard L. Evans (1906–1971)

The key is taking responsibility and initiative, deciding what your life is about and prioritizing your life around the most important things.

—Stephen R. Covey (1932–2012)

You will come to know that what appears today to be a sacrifice will prove instead to be the greatest investment that you will ever make.

—Gordon B. Hinckley (1910–2008)

Greatness is not always a matter of the scale of one's life, but of the quality of one's life. True greatness is not always tied to the scope of our tasks, but to the quality of how we carry out our tasks whatever they are. In that attitude, let us give our time, ourselves, and our talents to the things that really matter.

—Spencer W. Kimball (1895–1985)

If someone told you by digging long enough in a certain spot you would find a diamond of unmeasured wealth, do you think you would begrudge time or strength, or means spent to obtain that treasure? . . . If you will dig in the depths of your own hearts you will find, with the aid of the Spirit of the Lord, the pearl of great price, the testimony of the truth of this work.

—Zina D. H. Young (1821–1901)

When our minds really catch hold of the significance of Jesus' atonement, the world's hold on us loosens.

—Neal A. Maxwell (1926–2004)

At the end of your lives you will not be judged by academic successes, the degrees or diplomas earned, the positions held, the material wealth acquired, or power and prestige, but rather on the basis of what you have become as persons and what you are in conduct and character.

—Howard W. Hunter (1907–1995)

I would not give the ashes of a rye straw for any religion that was not worth living for and that was not worth dying for; and I would not give much for the man that was not willing to sacrifice his all for the sake of his religion.

—Lorenzo Snow (1814–1901)

WAR & PEACE

Perhaps nothing reveals the destructive capabilities of humanity as clearly as war. The devastation that war brings to individuals, families, and nations is seemingly without limit. And yet, despite the universal human desire for peace, we as humans seem unable permanently to leave war behind us.

An 1833 revelation to Joseph Smith, the founder of Mormonism, commanded the Latter-day Saints to "renounce war and proclaim peace" (Doctrine & Covenants 98:16). At the time, Mormons in Missouri were facing mob violence.

Mormon scriptures describe circumstances in which God's people are justified in going to

war, and Mormons in every nation are counseled to obey the law of the land in which they
live. This includes service in the armed services
where appropriate. At the same time, the goal
of working toward peace in the world—and
peace in individual families and lives—remains
constant.

Some, in speaking of war and troubles, will say, are you not afraid? No, I am a servant of God, and this is enough, for Father is at the helm. It is for me to be as clay in the hands of the potter, to be pliable and walk in the light of the countenance of the Spirit of the Lord, and then no matter what comes. Let the lightnings flash and the earthquakes bellow, God is at the helm.
—John Taylor (1808–1887)

And it came to pass that he rent his coat; and he took a piece thereof, and wrote upon it—In memory of our God, our religion, and freedom, and our peace, our wives, and our children—and he fastened it upon the end of a pole....

And when Moroni had said these words, he went forth among the people, waving the rent part of his garment in the air, that all might see the writing which he had written upon the rent part, and crying with a loud voice, saying:

Behold, whosoever will maintain this title upon the land, let them come forth in the strength of the Lord, and enter into a covenant that they will maintain their rights, and their religion, that the Lord God may bless them.

—Book of Mormon, Alma 46:12, 19–20

We repeat our warnings against the terrifying arms race in which the nations of the earth are presently engaged. We deplore in particular the building of vast arsenals of nuclear weaponry. We are advised that there is already enough such weaponry to destroy in large measure our civilization, with consequent suffering and misery of incalculable extent.

—First Presidency statement (May 5, 1981)

As citizens we are all under the direction of our respective national leaders. They have access to greater political and military intelligence than do the people generally. Those in the armed services are under obligation to their respective governments to execute the will of the sovereign. . . .

Even when the armaments of war ring out in deathly serenade and darkness and hatred reign in the hearts of some, there stands immovable, reassuring, comforting, and with great out-reaching love the quiet figure of the Son of God, the Redeemer of the world.

—Gordon B. Hinckley (1910–2008)

We need a more peaceful world, growing out of more peaceful families and neighborhoods and communities. To secure and cultivate such peace, we must love others, even our enemies as well as our friends. The world needs the gospel of Jesus Christ. Those who are filled with the love of Christ do not seek to force others to do better; they inspire others to do better, indeed inspire them to the pursuit of God. We need to extend the hand of friendship. We need to be kinder, more gentle, more forgiving, and slower to anger. We need to love one another with the pure love of Christ. May this be our course and our desire.

—Howard W. Hunter (1907–1995)

We believe firmly that the basis upon which world peace may be permanently obtained is not by sowing seeds of distrust and suspicion in people's minds; not by engendering enmity and hatred in human hearts; not by individuals or nations arrogating to themselves the claim of possessing all wisdom, or the only culture worth having; not by war with resulting suffering and death from submarines, poison gas, or explosions of nuclear bombs. No! The peace that will be permanent must be founded upon the principles of righteousness as taught and exemplified by the Prince of Peace, our Lord and Savior, Jesus Christ.

—David O. McKay (1873–1970)

Only to the extent that men desire peace and brotherhood can the world be made better. No peace, even though temporarily obtained, will be permanent, whether to individuals or nations, unless it is built upon the solid foundation of eternal principles.

—David O. McKay (1873–1970)

When enemies rise up, we commit vast resources to the fabrication of gods of stone and steel—ships, planes, missiles, fortifications—and depend on them for protection and deliverance. When threatened, we become antienemy instead of pro-kingdom of God; we train a man in the art of war and call him a patriot, thus, in the manner of Satan's counterfeit of true patriotism, perverting the Savior's teaching.

—Spencer W. Kimball (1895–1985)

We must be trained to clarify minds, heal broken hearts, and create homes where sunshine will make an environment in which mental and spiritual health may be nurtured. . . . Our schooling must not only teach us how to bridge the Niagara River gorge, or the Golden Gate, but must teach us how to bridge the deep gaps of misunderstanding and hate and discord in the world.

—Spencer W. Kimball (1895–1985)

PERSISTENCE &
IMPROVEMENT

Many Latter-day Saints tend to be goal-ori-
ented and spend a considerable amount of their
lives working toward self-improvement. This is
also the focus of many LDS Church teachings
and programs. In fact, one official objective of
the Church is to "perfect the Saints," meaning
to help members progress toward lifelong goals
of drawing closer to what God wants us to be.

Such progress requires ongoing effort. Latter-
day Saints constantly encourage each other
to "endure to the end." This includes not just
gritting your teeth and taking what life dishes
out to you but also pushing forward to achieve
your goals. Persistence in striving, in the
Mormon view, leads to true improvement—

both professionally and personally. And that's a big part of what life's all about (see **Divine Potential; Purpose of Life**).

—m—

Whether a man remains satisfied within what we designate the animal world, satisfied with what the animal world will give him, yielding without effort to the whim of his appetites and passions and slipping farther and farther into the realm of indulgence, or whether, through self-mastery, he rises toward intellectual, moral, and spiritual enjoyments depends upon the kind of choice he makes every day, nay, every hour of his life.

—David O. McKay (1873–1970)

The most important of all the commandments of God is that one that you are having the most difficulty keeping today.

—Harold B. Lee (1899–1973)

Success is never final.

—J. Willard Marriott (1900–1985)

Regardless of the adversities of life and the difficulties encountered in striving faithfully to endure, success can be achieved. . . . This, we can and must do if we would enjoy the blessings promised by the Lord to those who endure to the end.

—Belle S. Spafford (1895–1982)

I would crave as the richest of heaven's blessings . . . wisdom from my Heavenly Father bestowed daily, so that whatever I might do or say, I could not look back at the close of the day with regret, nor neglect the performance of any act that would bring a blessing.

—Emma Hale Smith (1804–1879)

Perseverance means to continue in a given course until we have reached a goal or objective, regardless of obstacles, opposition, and other counterinfluences. . . . Perseverance is a positive, active characteristic. . . . It gives us hope by helping us realize that the righteous suffer no failure except in giving up and no longer trying.
—Joseph B. Wirthlin (1917–2008)

Ideals are stars to steer by; they are not sticks to beat ourselves with.
—Barbara B. Smith (1922–2010)

Working toward perfection is not a one-time decision but a process to be pursued throughout one's lifetime.
—Spencer W. Kimball (1895–1985)

The only way I could overcome the pull of worldly tasks and personal pain was to cross the border of humanness into beauty and holiness by putting on the beautiful garment of his grace. The real borders are the walls of our own minds—the fears, the prejudice, the pull of daily concerns, the lack of acknowledgment to him who can so enlarge us with grace that we have Zion minds, pure and holy.

—Carol Clark Ottesen (1930–2006)

Some habits of ineffectiveness are rooted in our social conditioning toward quick-fix, short-term thinking.

—Stephen R. Covey (1932–2012)

Life is eternal. You are your own constant companion through every day of life and throughout all eternity. You cannot escape yourself. You could make choices that might give you a thrill for the moment, but what will be the lasting result?

—Camilla Eyring Kimball (1894–1987)

We need to allow for the enormous potential that each human being has.

—Emma Lou Thayne (1924–2014)

Rise to the great potential within you. I do not ask that you reach beyond your capacity. I hope you will not nag yourselves with thoughts of failure. I hope you will not try to set goals far beyond your capacity to achieve. I hope you will simply do what you can do in the best way you know how. If you do so, you will witness miracles come to pass.

—Gordon B. Hinckley (1910–2008)

Patience stoutly resists pulling up the daisies to see how the roots are doing.

—Neal A. Maxwell (1926–2004)

Each minute is a little thing, and yet, with respect to our personal productivity, to manage the minute is the secret of success.

—Joseph B. Wirthlin (1917–2008)

The men and women who desire to obtain seats in the celestial kingdom will find that they must battle every day.

—Brigham Young (1801–1877)

Everywhere in nature we are taught the lessons of patience and waiting. We want things a long time before we get them, and the fact that we want them a long time makes them all the more precious when they come.

—Joseph F. Smith (1838–1919)

Every individual can improve from day to day, from year to year, and have greater capacity to do things as the years come and the years go.

—Heber J. Grant (1856–1945)

Dream beautiful dreams and then work to make those dreams come true.

—Spencer W. Kimball (1895–1985)

If we keep doing what we're doing, we're going to keep getting what we're getting.

   —Stephen R. Covey (1932–2012)

How could a person possibly become what he is not thinking? Nor is any thought, when persistently entertained, too small to have its effect. The "divinity that shapes our ends" is indeed in ourselves.

   —Spencer W. Kimball (1895–1985)

While waiting for promised blessings, one should not mark time, for to fail to move forward is to some degree a retrogression. Be anxiously engaged in good causes, including your own development.

   —Howard W. Hunter (1907–1995)

Think about your particular assignment at this time in your life. It may be to get an education, it may be to rear children, it may be to be a grandparent, it may be to care for and relieve the suffering of someone you love, it may be to do a job in the most excellent way possible, it may be to support someone who has a difficult assignment of their own. Our assignments are varied and they change from time to time. Don't take them lightly. Give them your full heart and energy. Do them with enthusiasm. Do whatever you have to do this week with your whole heart and soul. To do less than this will leave you with an empty feeling.

—Marjorie Pay Hinckley (1911–2004)

The men and the women who are honest before God, who humbly plod along, doing their duty . . . and who help look after the poor; and who honor the holy priesthood, who do not run into excesses, who are prayerful in their families, and who acknowledge the Lord in their hearts, they will build up a foundation that the gates of hell cannot prevail against.

—Joseph F. Smith (1838–1919)

Wherefore, ye must press forward with a steadfastness in Christ, having a perfect brightness of hope, and a love of God and of all men. Wherefore, if ye shall press forward, feasting upon the word of Christ, and endure to the end, behold, thus saith the Father: Ye shall have eternal life.

—Book of Mormon, 3 Nephi 31:20

PRAYER

Mormons, like believers from every faith, believe in prayer. Each Mormon church meeting begins and ends with prayer. Mormons pray in their families and over meals. Children are taught from an early age to pray individually, using their own words to express the thoughts of their hearts but following the general pattern of first addressing God ("Dear Heavenly Father," or something similar); giving thanks for blessings; asking for help as needed; and closing in the name of Jesus Christ.

Prayer, in the Mormon view, is an act of devotion, but also much more. It is communication with a loving Heavenly Father (see **Heavenly Parents**). It is a chance to review successes and make plans for the future—a kind of personal interview. It is a chance to seek revelation and inspiration. It is a refuge from the storms of the world, a lifeline to heaven, and a chance to be reminded about those things that matter most.

—⚬⚬⚬—

Were I to draw a distinction in all the duties that are required of the children of men, from first to last, I would place first and foremost the duty of seeking unto the Lord our God until we open the path of communication from heaven to earth.

—Brigham Young (1801–1877)

Cry unto [God] for mercy; for he is mighty to save.

Yea, humble yourselves, and continue in prayer unto him.

Cry unto him when ye are in your fields, yea, over all your flocks.

Cry unto him in your houses, yea, over all your household, both morning, mid-day, and evening.

Yea, cry unto him against the power of your enemies.

Yea, cry unto him against the devil, who is an enemy to all righteousness.

Cry unto him over the crops of your fields, that ye may prosper in them.

Cry over the flocks of your fields, that they may increase.

But this is not all; ye must pour out your souls in your closets, and your secret places, and in your wilderness.

Yea, and when you do not cry unto the Lord, let your hearts be full, drawn out in prayer unto him continually for your welfare, and also for the welfare of those who are around you.

—Book of Mormon, Alma 34:18-27

The straight and narrow path, though clearly marked, is a path, not a freeway nor an escalator. Indeed, there are times when the only way the straight and narrow path can be followed is on one's knees.

—Neal A. Maxwell (1926–2004)

It matters not whether you or I feel like praying, when the time comes to pray, pray. If we do not feel like it, we should pray till we do.

—Brigham Young (1801–1877)

The best way to obtain truth and wisdom is not to ask from books, but to go to God in prayer, and obtain divine teaching.

—Joseph Smith (1805–1844)

When I am angry, the *first* thing I do is pray. And I am never so angry but what I can't.

—Heber C. Kimball (1801–1868)

The minute a man stops supplicating God for his Spirit and direction, just so soon he starts out to become a stranger to him and his works. When men stop praying for God's Spirit, they place confidence in their own unaided reason, and they gradually lose the Spirit of God.

—Heber J. Grant (1856–1945)

You must study it out in your mind; then you must ask me if it be right, and if it is right I will cause that your bosom shall burn within you; therefore, you shall feel that it is right. But if it be not right you shall have no such feelings, but you shall have a stupor of thought that shall cause you to forget the thing which is wrong.

—Doctrine & Covenants 9:8–9

There are many reasons our prayers may lack power. Sometimes they become routine. Our prayers become hollow when we say similar words in similar ways over and over so often that the words become more of a recitation than a communication.

—Joseph B. Wirthlin (1917–2008)

I find that when I get casual in my relationships with divinity and when it seems that no divine ear is listening and no divine voice is speaking, that I am far, far away. If I immerse myself in the scriptures the distance narrows and the spirituality returns.

—Spencer W. Kimball (1895–1985)

In the quiet hours, in the heat of battle, and through the hazards of the day; in times of temptation, of sorrow, of peace and of blessing, let us pray always, both alone, and with our families gathered around us, with gratitude for the blessings of life, for understanding of its problems, and for strength to endure to the end.
—Heber J. Grant (1856–1945)

The young man who closes the door behind him, who draws the curtains, and there in silence pleads with God for help, should first pour out his soul in gratitude for health, for friends, for loved ones, for the gospel, for the manifestations of God's existence. He should first count his many blessings and name them one by one.

—David O. McKay (1873–1970)

Prayer is a great tower of strength, a pillar of unending righteousness, a mighty force that moves mountains and saves souls. Through it the sick are healed, the dead are raised, and the Holy Spirit is poured out without measure upon the faithful.

—Bruce R. McConkie (1915–1985)

Pray always, and I will pour out my Spirit upon you, and great shall be your blessing—yea, even more than if you should obtain treasures of earth.

—Doctrine & Covenants 19:38

We pay too little attention to the value of meditation, a principle of devotion. In our worship there are two elements: One is spiritual communion arising from our own meditation; the other, instruction from others, particularly from those who have authority to guide and instruct us. Of the two, the more profitable introspectively is the meditation. Meditation is the language of the soul. It is defined as "a form of private devotion, or spiritual exercise, consisting in deep, continued reflection on some religious theme." Meditation is a form of prayer.

—David O. McKay (1873–1970)

OBEDIENCE

Popular films sometimes depict churchgoers gathered in crowded pews on a hot Sunday afternoon while a stern and impassioned preacher stands high on his pulpit, warning of hellfire and damnation to those who disobey God. Indeed, the Bible is rife with passages urging all to "fear" God.

In contrast, Latter-day Saint teachings explain that fear of God is often misinterpreted. According to the bible dictionary in the LDS edition of the King James Bible, "The 'fear of the Lord' is frequently spoken of as part of man's duty.... In such passages fear is equivalent to reverence, awe, worship, and is therefore an essential part of the attitude of mind in which we ought to stand toward the all-holy God."

With this interpretation in mind, Mormons are taught that obedience to God is not a burden but a joy, because it brings peace of mind and immeasurable blessings poured out by a loving Heavenly Father in order to help us achieve our potential (see **Heavenly Parents**; **Divine Potential**). Most Mormons believe that obedience to God's commandments leads to a degree of freedom and happiness that could not otherwise be obtained.

—◊◊◊—

He who doeth the works of righteousness shall receive his reward, even peace in this world, and eternal life in the world to come.

—Doctrine & Covenants 59:23

For the natural man is an enemy to God, and has been from the fall of Adam, and will be, forever and ever, unless he yields to the enticings of the Holy Spirit, and putteth off the natural man and becometh a saint through the atonement of Christ the Lord, and becometh as a child, submissive, meek, humble, patient, full of love, willing to submit to all things which the Lord seeth fit to inflict upon him, even as a child doth submit to his father.

—Book of Mormon, Mosiah 3:19

When obedience ceases to be an irritant and becomes our quest, in that moment God will endow us with power.

—Ezra Taft Benson (1899–1994)

I desire the Spirit of God to know and understand myself, that I might be able to overcome whatever of tradition or nature that would not tend to my exaltation in the eternal worlds.

—Emma Hale Smith (1804–1879)

When God commands, do it.

—Joseph Smith (1805–1844)

Obedience brings peace in decision-making. If we have firmly made up our minds to follow the commandments, we will not have to redecide which path to take when temptation comes our way.

—James E. Faust (1920–2007)

Men and women who turn their lives over to God will discover that he can make a lot more out of their lives than they can. He will deepen their joys, expand their vision, quicken their minds, strengthen their muscles, lift their spirits, multiply their blessings, increase their opportunities, comfort their souls, raise up friends, and pour out peace. Whoever will lose his life in the service of God will find eternal life.

—Ezra Taft Benson (1899–1994)

A religion that does not require the sacrifice of all things never has the power sufficient to produce the faith necessary unto life and salvation.

—Joseph Smith (1805–1844)

The submission of one's will is really the only uniquely personal thing we have to place on God's altar. The many other things we "give," brothers and sisters, are actually the things he has already given or loaned to us. However, when you and I finally submit ourselves, by letting our individual wills be swallowed up in God's will, then we are really giving something to him! It is the only possession which is truly ours to give!

—Neal A. Maxwell (1926–2004)

The great test of life is obedience to God.

—Ezra Taft Benson (1899–1994)

Being bridled, or yielding obediently to restraint, is necessary for our personal growth and progression.

—James E. Faust (1920–2007)

How shall we know that we obey [God]? There is but one method by which we can know it, and that is by the inspiration of the Spirit of the Lord witnessing unto our spirit that we are his, that we love him, and that he loves us. It is by the spirit of revelation we know this.

—Brigham Young (1801–1877)

We believe that worship is far more than prayer and preaching and gospel performance. The supreme act of worship is to keep the commandments, to follow in the footsteps of the Son of God, to do ever those things that please him. It is one thing to give lip service to the Lord; it is quite another to respect and honor his will by following the example he has set for us.

—Joseph Fielding Smith (1876–1972)

There are certain eternal laws by which the Gods in the eternal worlds are governed and which they cannot violate, and do not want to violate. These eternal principles must be kept, and one principle is that no unclean thing can enter into the kingdom of God.

—John Taylor (1808–1887)

No obstacles are insurmountable when God commands and we obey.

—Heber J. Grant (1856–1945)

If we are faithful in keeping the commandments of God, his promises will be fulfilled to the very letter. . . . The trouble is, the adversary of men's souls blinds their minds. He throws dust, so to speak, in their eyes, and they are blinded with the things of this world.

—Heber J. Grant (1856–1945)

There are two influences in the world. The one is the influence of our Heavenly Father and the other is the influence of Satan. We can take our choice which territory we want to live in, that of our Heavenly Father or that of Satan.

—George Albert Smith (1870–1951)

We believe it is by grace that we are saved after all that we can do, and that building upon the foundation of the atonement of Christ, all men must work out their salvation with fear and trembling before the Lord.

—Joseph Fielding Smith (1876–1972)

Disobedience is essentially a prideful power struggle against someone in authority over us. It can be a parent, a priesthood leader, a teacher, or ultimately God. A proud person hates the fact that someone is above him. He thinks this lowers his position.

—Ezra Taft Benson (1899–1994)

The great task of life is to learn the will of the Lord and then do it.

—Ezra Taft Benson (1899–1994)

There is a law, irrevocably decreed in heaven before the foundations of this world, upon which all blessings are predicated—and when we obtain any blessing from God, it is by obedience to that law upon which it is predicated.

—Doctrine & Covenants 130:20–21

When we put God first, all other things fall into their proper place or drop out of our lives.

—Ezra Taft Benson (1899–1994)

HEALTH

Mormons are instructed to live a clean and healthy lifestyle. Latter-day Saints have a strict code of health that they refer to as the "Word of Wisdom." Outside of the Church, the Word of Wisdom is commonly equated with things that Mormons are prohibited from consuming, including tea, coffee, alcohol, tobacco products, and other harmful drugs. Many Mormons also interpret the spirit of the Word of Wisdom as involving positive health practices as well, such as eating properly, exercising, getting appropriate rest and relaxation, and seeking medical care as appropriate.

Such guidelines have several purposes. For example, Mormons see maintaining a healthy body as a sign of respect for the gift of a physical body that God has granted to them. Avoiding addicting and mind-altering substances helps preserve freedom of choice and individual responsibility (see **Choices & Freedom**). And good health empowers individuals to make the most of positive opportunities, including service to others.

Mormons who follow the Word of Wisdom guidelines believe that by so doing, they "shall find wisdom and great treasures of knowledge, even hidden treasures; and shall run and not be weary, and shall walk and not faint" (Doctrine & Covenants 89:18–20).

—〰—

In consequence of evils and designs which do and will exist in the hearts of conspiring men in the last days, I have warned you, and forewarn you, by giving unto you this word of wisdom by revelation—that inasmuch as any man drinketh wine or strong drink among you, behold it is not good, neither meet in the sight of your Father. . . . And, again, strong drinks are not for the belly, but for the washing of your bodies. And again, tobacco is not for the body. . . . And again, hot drinks are not for the body or belly.

—Doctrine & Covenants 89:4–9

I was always very sickly until now. I had quit taking snuff, tea and coffee, and I became healthy and strong, when before I could not walk half a mile, now I could walk three miles and not tire, for we kept the Word of Wisdom.

—Drusilla Dorris Hendricks (1810–1881)

We receive numerous letters inquiring whether this item or that item is proscribed by the Word of Wisdom. If we will avoid those things which are definitely and specifically defined, and beyond this observe the spirit of that great revelation, it will not involve a burden. It will, rather, bring a blessing. Do not forget: it is the Lord who has made the promise.

—Gordon B. Hinckley (1910–2008)

The Americans as a nation are killing themselves with their vices and high living. . . . Dispense with your multitudinous dishes, and, depend upon it, you will do much towards preserving your families from sickness, disease and death.

—Brigham Young (1801–1877)

If you and I desire the blessings of life, of health, of vigor of body and mind; if we desire the destroying angel to pass us by, as he did in the days of the children of Israel, we must obey the Word of Wisdom; then God is bound, and the blessing shall come to us.

—Heber J. Grant (1856–1945)

The Word of Wisdom is a law—a principle with promise. If we obey the provisions of the law, we receive the promises. If we do not, there will be both temporal and spiritual consequences.

—Ezra Taft Benson (1899–1994)

It is difficult to find anything more healthy to drink than good cold water, such as flows down to us from springs and snows of our mountains. This is the beverage we should drink. It should be our drink at all times.

—Brigham Young (1801–1877)

What a wonderful thing it is, this Word of Wisdom. It doesn't impose burdens on us. It gives us blessings.

—Gordon B. Hinckley (1910–2008)

I recall a bishop telling me of a woman who came to him to get a temple recommend. When asked if she observed the Word of Wisdom, she said that she occasionally drank a cup of coffee. She said, "Now, Bishop, you're not going to let that keep me from going to the temple, are you?" To which he replied, "Sister, surely you will not let a cup of coffee stand between you and the house of the Lord."

—Gordon B. Hinckley (1910–2008)

Cease to be idle; cease to be unclean; cease to find fault one with another; cease to sleep longer than is needful; retire to thy bed early, that ye may not be weary; arise early, that your bodies and your minds may be invigorated.

—Doctrine & Covenants 88:124

With reference to cola drinks, the Church has never officially taken a position on the matter, but the leaders of the Church have advised, and we do specifically advise, against the use of any drink containing harmful habit-forming drugs under circumstances that would result in acquiring the habit. Any beverage that contains ingredients harmful to the body should be avoided.

—*Priesthood Bulletin* (1972)

The reward for keeping the Word of Wisdom is four-fold. (1) Self-control is developed. That is implied in verse three of the revelation which states that the Word of Wisdom is "adapted to the capacity of the weak and the weakest of all Saints, who are or can be called Saints." (2) Strength of body, including resistance to contagion, is a result of wise living. (3) Clearness of mind is the gift of those whose bodies are in a healthy condition. (4) Spiritual power comes to all who conquer their appetites, live normally, and look upward to God.

—John A. Widtsoe (1872–1952)

I look upon the Word of Wisdom as kind advice of our Father in heaven, who desires to see his children become more like him. . . . I take it as the fatherly counsel of one who, knowing what I needed, said to me: "My son, these things are not good for you, and if you will avoid them I will give you the companionship of my Holy Spirit and joy while you live in the world and in the end eternal life." How foolish I would be then to partake of these forbidden things, having the assurance that it is the counsel of the Lord I should abstain therefrom. . . . He who knows better than anybody else says that they are harmful, and has warned me against them.

—George Albert Smith (1870–1951)

All saints who remember to keep and do these sayings, walking in obedience to the commandments, shall receive health in their navel and marrow to their bones; and shall find wisdom and great treasures of knowledge, even hidden treasures; and shall run and not be weary, and shall walk and not faint.

—Doctrine & Covenants 89:18–20

LEADERSHIP

Unlike the leaders of many churches, the leadership of the Church of Jesus Christ of Latter-day Saints, on both a local and central level, is made up almost entirely of laypeople who earn or have earned a living by secular means. This means that Mormons often volunteer considerable time and energy to the roles and responsibilities of Church leadership.

Understandably, training Latter-day Saints in leadership skills receives considerable focus. From as early as age twelve, Church members are frequently called to lead and be led by others in a wide variety of Church organizations and functions. A typical Mormon may be called to lead in various capacities throughout his or her life.

Generally speaking, the LDS model of leadership prescribes leading others by example as opposed to force. By gentle invitation instead of stern dictates. By persuasion instead of coercion. By love and compassion, instead of dominance or charisma. Effective leaders delegate tasks, allowing others to shine according to their strengths. At times, they challenge others to stretch beyond their current capacities. Good leaders always thank and praise others for their contributions.

Above all else, being a good leader means serving those we direct, as Christ did.

—❦—

When you show deep empathy toward others, their defensive energy goes down, and positive energy replaces it. That's when you can get more creative in solving problems.

—Stephen R. Covey (1932–2012)

Jesus said several times, "Come, follow me." His was a program of "do what I do," rather than "do what I say." His innate brilliance would have permitted him to put on a dazzling display, but that would have left his followers far behind. He walked and worked with those he was to serve. His was not a long-distance leadership. He was not afraid of close friendships; he was not afraid that proximity to him would disappoint his followers. The leaven of true leadership cannot lift others unless we are with and serve those to be led.

—Spencer W. Kimball (1895–1985)

A leader must be a good listener. He must be willing to take counsel. He must show a genuine concern and love for those under his stewardship.

—James E. Faust (1920–2007)

Listen with the intent to understand, not the intent to reply.

—Stephen R. Covey (1932–2012)

No power or influence can or ought to be maintained by virtue of the priesthood, only by persuasion, by long-suffering, by gentleness and meekness, and by love unfeigned;

By kindness, and pure knowledge, which shall greatly enlarge the soul without hypocrisy, and without guile—

Reproving betimes with sharpness, when moved upon by the Holy Ghost; and then showing forth afterwards an increase of love toward him whom thou hast reproved, lest he esteem thee to be his enemy.

—Doctrine & Covenants 121:41–43

Note the qualities that the Lord demands of those who are to represent us. They must be good, wise, and honest.

—Ezra Taft Benson (1899–1994)

Leadership is not position. It's moral authority. Moral authority comes from following universal and timeless principles like honesty, integrity, treating people with respect.
— Stephen R. Covey (1932–2012)

Leaders are movers and shakers, original, inventive, unpredictable, imaginative, full of surprises that discomfit the enemy in war and the main office in peace. . . . The leader . . . has a passion for *equality*.
— Hugh Nibley (1910–2005)

Live every day of your lives . . . so that your examples may be worthy of imitation.
— Brigham Young (1801–1877)

When we undertake to cover our sins, or to gratify our pride, our vain ambition, or to exercise control or dominion or compulsion upon the souls of the children of men, in any degree of unrighteousness, behold, the heavens withdraw themselves; the Spirit of the Lord is grieved; and when it is withdrawn, Amen to the priesthood or the authority of that man.

—Doctrine & Covenants 121:37

I teach them correct principles, and they govern themselves.

—Joseph Smith (1805–1844)

WORK

The first Mormons—largely of New England Puritan stock—brought with them a commitment to work, not only as a way of getting ahead in the world, but also as a way of serving God. When the Mormon pioneers settled the Intermountain West, they chose as their symbol the beehive, representing organization, industry, and unity. Their hard work made the desert "blossom as the rose" (Isaiah 35:1).

Work, for Mormons, has spiritual as well as temporal importance, just as necessary for emotional health as prayer (see **Prayer**). In the Mormon view, heaven isn't a place where people sit and relax—it's a condition of joyful, fruitful work.

You can still see the beehive on highway signs and other places in Utah today.

—⚏—

For behold, this is my work and my glory—to bring to pass the immortality and eternal life of man.

—Pearl of Great Price, Moses 39:1

The best antidote I know for worry is work.

—Gordon B. Hinckley (1910–2008)

Forget yourself and go to work.

—Bryant S. Hinckley (1867–1961)

Work is a spiritual necessity as well as an economic necessity.

—Spencer W. Kimball (1895–1985)

Our primary purpose [in establishing the Church's welfare program] was to set up, in so far as it might be possible, a system under which the curse of idleness would be done away with, the evils of a dole abolished, and independence, industry, thrift and self respect be once more established amongst our people. The aim of the Church is to help the people to help themselves. Work is to be re-enthroned as the ruling principle of the lives of our Church membership.

—Heber J. Grant (1856–1945)

Work brings happiness, self-esteem, and prosperity. It is the means of all accomplishment; it is the opposite of idleness. . . . Attempts to obtain our temporal, social, emotional, or spiritual well-being by means of a dole violate the divine mandate that we should work for what we receive.

—Spencer W. Kimball (1895–1985)

Of the time that is allotted to man here on the earth there is none to lose or to run to waste. After suitable rest and relaxation there is not a day, hour or minute that we should spend in idleness, but every minute of every day of our lives we should strive to improve our minds and to increase the faith of the holy Gospel.

—Brigham Young (1801–1877)

The privilege to work is a gift, the power to work is a blessing, the love of work is success.

—David O. McKay (1873–1970)

Daydreams without work do not amount to anything; it is the actual work that counts.

—Heber J. Grant (1856–1945)

There is no substitute under the heavens for productive labor. It is the process by which dreams become realities. It is the process by which idle visions become dynamic achievements.

—Gordon B. Hinckley (1910–2008)

There is a heavy emphasis in Mormonism on initiative, on responsibility, on a work ethic, and on education. If you take those elements together with a free-enterprise system, you've got the chemistry for a lot of industry.

—Stephen R. Covey (1932–2012)

If we are to be saved in an ark, as Noah and his family were, it will be because we build it. . . . My faith does not lead me to think the Lord will provide us with roast pigs, bread already buttered, etc.; he will give us the ability to raise the grain, to obtain the fruits of the earth, to make habitations, to procure a few boards to make a box, and when harvest comes, giving us the grain, it is for us to preserve it—to save the wheat until we have one, two, five or seven years' provisions on hand, until there is enough of the staff of life saved by the people to bread themselves and those who will come here seeking for safety.

— Brigham Young (1801–1877)

If you have ambitions, dream of what you wish to accomplish, and then put your shoulder to the wheel and work.

—Heber J. Grant (1856–1945)

It is not so much what we know that is important, as what we are and what we do.
        —Spencer W. Kimball (1895–1985)

The most important work you'll ever do is ahead of you, never behind you.
        —Stephen R. Covey (1932–2012)

SELF-RELIANCE

"God helps them who help themselves," the aphorism goes. Mormons seem to believe it. The subjects of avoiding debt, emergency preparedness, food storage, and self-reliance seem to come up, in one form or another, almost every time the LDS Church holds its twice-yearly general conference, a televised event in which the Church's highest-ranking leaders address all Mormons worldwide. In fact, the topics are discussed so frequently that some have called Latter-day Saints doomsday preppers—and perhaps not without good reason.

Why this heavy emphasis on self-reliance? The reasons are varied. Debt is seen as a form of servitude, something that robs a person of his or her free will (see **Choices & Freedom**). A supply of food and other necessities in time of natural disaster or public emergency could mean the difference between life and death for a person and his or her loved ones. Preparation also helps us weather personal difficulties, such as loss of employment. Where possible, Mormons don't want to be a burden on others.

Perhaps most importantly, *Latter-day* Saints, as the name implies, believe in being prepared for the last days of the world, the time in which Jesus Christ himself will return to reign over all humankind. While Mormons do not claim knowledge of the specific time of Christ's arrival, they believe upheavals will happen beforehand, and blessings will come to those who are prepared.

—∿—

For the moment we live in a day of peace and prosperity, but it shall not ever be thus. Great trials lie ahead . . . and we must prepare ourselves temporally and spiritually.

—Bruce R. McConkie (1915–1985)

How on the face of the earth could a man enjoy his religion, when he had been told by the Lord how to prepare for a day of famine, when, instead of doing so, he had fooled away that which would have sustained him and his family.

—George A. Smith (1817–1875)

Let every head of every household see to it that he has on hand enough food and clothing, and, where possible, fuel also, for at least a year ahead. . . . Let every head of every household aim to own his own home, free from mortgage. Let every man who has a garden spot, garden it; every man who owns a farm, farm it.

—J. Reuben Clark (1871–1961)

Maintain a year's supply. The Lord has urged that his people save for the rainy days, prepare for the difficult times, and put away for emergencies, a year's supply or more of bare necessities so that when comes the flood, the earthquake, the famine, the hurricane, the storms of life, our families can be sustained through the dark days.
—Spencer W. Kimball (1895–1985)

As we have been continuously counseled for more than sixty years, let us have some food set aside that would sustain us for a time in case of need. But let us not panic nor go to extremes. Let us be prudent in every respect.
—Gordon B. Hinckley (1910–2008)

Self-reliance is not the end, but a means to an end. It is very possible for a person to be completely independent and lack every other desirable attribute. One may become wealthy and never have to ask anyone for anything, but unless there is some spiritual goal attached to this independence, it can canker his soul.

—Marion G. Romney (1897–1988)

Too often we bask in our comfortable complacency and rationalize that the ravages of war, economic disaster, famine, and earthquake cannot happen here. Those who believe this are either not acquainted with the revelations of the Lord, or they do not believe them. Those who smugly think these calamities will not happen, that they will somehow be set aside because of the righteousness of the Saints, are deceived and will rue the day they harbored such a delusion.

—Ezra Taft Benson (1899–1994)

When we really get into hard times, where food is scarce or there is none at all, and so with clothing and shelter, money may be no good for there may be nothing to buy, and you cannot eat money, you cannot get enough of it together to burn to keep you warm, and you cannot wear it.
—J. Reuben Clark (1871–1961)

There is more salvation and security in wheat than in all the political schemes of the world.
—Orson Hyde (1805–1878)

The time will come that gold will hold no comparison in value to a bushel of wheat.
—Brigham Young (1801–1877)

Grow all the food that you feasibly can on your own property. Berry bushes, grapevines, fruit trees—plant them if your climate is right for their growth. Grow vegetables and eat them from your own yard.

—Spencer W. Kimball (1895–1985)

Let us be in a position so we are able to not only feed ourselves through home production and storage, but others as well.

—Ezra Taft Benson (1899–1994)

If ye are prepared ye shall not fear.

—Doctrine & Covenants 38:30

KINDNESS &
ACCEPTANCE

No one would deny that religious belief has been used at times as an excuse for intolerance and cruelty. Clearly, however, that's not the way it's supposed to be. Virtually every religious tradition teaches kindness toward others, and Mormonism is no exception.

According to Mormon doctrine, all people are literal spiritual sisters and brothers, sons and daughters of loving heavenly parents. As such, we each have a duty to love and care for one another as we would for members of our own earthly families.

Are Mormons perfect at applying these principles in our lives? Hardly. Perhaps that's one reason why Church talks and lessons—not to mention the scriptures—address these topics so often.

—⅏—

Don't try to tear down other people's religion about their ears. Build up your own perfect structure of truth, and invite your listeners to enter in and enjoy its glories.

—Brigham Young (1801–1877)

No greater reward can come to any of us as we serve than a sincere "Thank you for being my friend."

—Marvin J. Ashton (1915–1994)

Never suppress a generous thought.

—Camilla Eyring Kimball (1894–1987)

Borders are of our own making and . . . if we are to truly become brothers and sisters, we must seek his grace to move into the realm of holiness.

—Carol Clark Ottesen (1930–2006)

The bonds of the gospel . . . transcend time and trial, uniting sisters now as then in a oneness of faith. . . .

Example after example comes from women in many places, from women of greatly differing circumstances in life—women alone, women with children, women old, women young, women new to the Church, women in sorrow, women in despair, women happy.

They form a mosaic of many lives with differing circumstances, with individual talents, and with gifts wonderfully varied. The details of each life are so numerous that we begin to see in them the great diversity among us, and with it great strength and enrichment.

—Barbara B. Smith (1922–2010)

If you have a granary full of grain, and you give away a sack or two, there remain that many less in your granary, but if you perform a kind act or add words of encouragement to one in distress, who is struggling along in the battle of life, the greater is your capacity to do this in the future. Don't go through life with your lips sealed against words of kindness and encouragement, nor your hearts sealed against performing labors for another. Make a motto in life: always try and assist someone else to carry his burden.

—Heber J. Grant (1856–1945)

Let us be sensitive to the unchanging and powerful core principles of the gospel. Let us understand that they matter most. Let us build firm foundations on these principles. Then when the rains fall and the floods come, our house will be "founded upon a rock" and it will not fall (Matt. 7:25). Then, building on that firm foundation, let us rejoice with each other, listen to each other, learn from each other, and help each other apply those principles as we deal with our different circumstances, different cultures, different generations, and different geographies.

—Chieko N. Okazaki (1926–2011)

No matter in what land we may dwell the Gospel of the Lord Jesus Christ makes us brothers and sisters, interested in each other, eager to understand and know each other.

—Heber J. Grant (1856–1945)

I would not be an enemy to any living soul.

—George Albert Smith (1870–1951)

You cannot drive people to do things which are right, but you can love them into doing them, if your example is of such a character that they can see you mean what you say.

—George Albert Smith (1870–1951)

Look for good in men, and where they fail to possess it, try to build it up in them; try to increase the good in them; look for the good; build up the good; sustain the good; and speak as little about the evil as you possibly can.

—Joseph F. Smith (1838–1919)

One who is kind is sympathetic and gentle with others. He is considerate of others' feelings and courteous in his behavior. He has a helpful nature. Kindness pardons others' weaknesses and faults. Kindness is extended to all—to the aged and the young, to animals, to those low of station as well as the high.

—Ezra Taft Benson (1899–1994)

This Christmas, mend a quarrel. Seek out a forgotten friend. Dismiss suspicion and replace it with trust. Write a letter. Give a soft answer. Encourage youth. Manifest your loyalty in word and deed. Keep a promise. Forgo a grudge. Forgive an enemy. Apologize. Try to understand. Examine your demands on others. Think first of someone else. Be kind. Be gentle. Laugh a little more. Express your gratitude. Welcome a stranger. Gladden the heart of a child. Take pleasure in the beauty and wonder of the earth. Speak your love and then speak it again.

—Howard W. Hunter (1907–1995)

We need to remember that though we make our friends, God has made our neighbors— everywhere. Love should have no boundary; we should have no narrow loyalties.

—Howard W. Hunter (1907–1995)

Love is the security for which children weep, the yearning of youth, the adhesive that binds marriage, and the lubricant that prevents devastating friction in the home; it is the peace of old age, the sunlight of hope shining through death. How rich are those who enjoy it in their associations with family, friends, and neighbors! Love, like faith, is a gift of God. It is also the most enduring and most powerful virtue.
—Gordon B. Hinckley (1910–2008)

We're all sons and daughters of God, and therefore in a very literal sense, brothers and sisters. And we ought to treat each other that way.
—Gordon B. Hinckley (1910–2008)

Strength lies in differences, not in similarities.
—Stephen R. Covey (1932–2012)

Nothing is so much calculated to lead people to forsake sin as to take them by the hand and to watch over them with tenderness. When persons manifest the least kindness and love to me, O what pow'r it has over my mind.

—Joseph Smith (1805–1844)

Oh, how we need each other. Those of us who are old need you who are young. And, hopefully, you who are young need some of us who are old. . . . We need deep and satisfying and loyal friendships with each other.

—Marjorie Pay Hinckley (1911–2004)

The worst sinners, according to Jesus, are not the harlots and publicans, but the religious leaders with their insistence on proper dress and grooming, their careful observance of all the rules, their precious concern for status symbols, their strict legality, their pious patriotism. . . . The haircut becomes the test of virtue in a world where Satan deceives and rules by appearances.

—Hugh Nibley (1910–2005)

When at length we tire of putting people down, this self-inflicted fatigue can give way to the invigorating calisthenics of lifting people up

—Neal A. Maxwell (1926–2004)

The deepest hunger of the human body is air. The deepest hunger of the human heart is to feel understood.

—Stephen R. Covey (1932–2012)

When . . . great individuals move so marvelously along the straight and narrow path, it is unseemly of us to call attention to the fact that one of their shoelaces is untied as they make the journey.

—Neal A. Maxwell (1926–2004)

The true greatness of a person, in my view, is evident in the way he or she treats those where courtesy and kindness are not required.

—Joseph B. Wirthlin (1917–2008)

SERVICE &
CHARITY

People often use the word *charity* in talking about philanthropy and humanitarian efforts. For Mormons, these things, while spiritually elevating pursuits, are only a small portion of what makes up the virtue of charity. In its simplest form, members of the LDS faith interpret charity as "the pure love of Christ" (Book of Mormon, Moroni 7:47). While charity manifests itself perhaps most often through acts of service, it is more than just random acts of kindness. It's a character trait. An attribute. An all-encompassing attitude of compassion and kindness toward others, born from a desire to love others as Christ did.

In Mormonism, serving others is akin to serving God. Furthermore, to serve others is to gradually become more like him (see **Purpose of Life**). Latter-day Saints see Jesus Christ as the ultimate exemplar of charity. Service must be performed willingly and selflessly for it to be of the greatest benefit. Acts of charity that are performed grudgingly, while better than nothing, fall short of the maximum potential for blessings promised by God.

All followers of Christ who devote their lives to charitable acts of service toward their fellow man are promised, as the New Testament proclaims, that they shall be saved (see Luke 17:33).

—⟶⟵—

It seems to be that, of all our learning, that which we obtain by way of giving compassionately is the most significant learning we ever do.
—Barbara B. Smith (1922–2010)

God does notice us, and he watches over us. But it is usually through another person that he meets our needs.
—Spencer W. Kimball (1895–1985)

Selflessness is a key to happiness and effectiveness; it is precious and must be preserved as a virtue which guarantees so many other virtues.
—Spencer W. Kimball (1895–1985)

Sisterhood is made glorious by the often unheralded efforts of local women to serve the Lord quietly, looking to the needs of neighbors, tenderly serving at the time of a death, faithfully filling assignments in Church organizations, selflessly improving conditions in their communities, courageously teaching and defending the truth, steadfastly supporting the priesthood, and, with all, creating loving homes where his spirit may dwell.

—Barbara B. Smith (1922–2010)

I have just found out how the widow's crust and barrel held out through the famine. Just as it was out, someone was sent to fill it.

—Drusilla Dorris Hendricks (1810–1881)

You exert a certain degree of influence, and be it ever so small, it affects some person or persons, and for the results of the influence you exert you are held more or less accountable. You, therefore, whether you acknowledge it or not, have assumed an importance before God and man that cannot be overlooked.

—Lorenzo Snow (1814–1901)

The genuine mother takes time to reach out beyond her own children and sense her responsibility to help all children. Wherever a child is found cold, hungry, or in need of attention or care of any kind, a good mother will render loving and intelligent service.

—Camilla Eyring Kimball (1894–1987)

Jesus saw sin as wrong but also was able to see sin as springing from deep and unmet needs on the part of the sinner.

—Spencer W. Kimball (1895–1985)

The principle of love within us is an attribute of the Deity, and it is placed within us to be dispensed independently according to our own will.

—Brigham Young (1801–1877)

There are many opportunities for service to others. The world is full of lonely, troubled people who need a helping hand, who need a listening ear or a friendly visit or a comforting letter. Our watchword should be "Never stop growing and serving."

—Camilla Eyring Kimball (1894–1987)

Let us not forget the obligation which rests upon us to render allegiance and service to the Lord, and that acceptable service to him cannot be rendered without service to our fellow man.

—Heber J. Grant (1856–1945)

The greatest thing in the world is love. And if we keep that always in our hearts, and give it as a message to those about us, we will be blessed and will be instruments in blessing those with whom we associate.

—Clarissa Smith Williams (1859–1930)

Our eternal happiness will be in proportion to the way that we devote ourselves to helping others.

—George Albert Smith (1870–1951)

True happiness comes only by making others happy—the practical application of the Savior's doctrine of losing one's life to gain it. In short, the Christmas spirit is the Christ spirit that makes our hearts glow in brotherly love and friendship and prompts us to kind deeds of service.

—David O. McKay (1873–1970)

My life is like my shoes—to be worn out in service.
—Spencer W. Kimball (1895–1985)

It is clear that plans which contemplate only relieving present distress are deficient. . . . Our idea of charity, therefore, is to relieve present wants and then to put the poor in a way to help themselves so that in turn they may help others.
—Joseph F. Smith (1838–1919)

You cannot lift another soul until you are standing on higher ground than he is. You cannot light a fire in another soul unless it is burning in your own soul.
—Harold B. Lee (1899–1973)

The more we serve our fellowmen in appropriate ways, the more substance there is to our souls. We become more significant individuals as we serve others. We become more substantive as we serve others—indeed, it is easier to "find" ourselves because there is so much more of us to find!

—Spencer W. Kimball (1895–1985)

If ye have not charity, ye are nothing, for charity never faileth. Wherefore, cleave unto charity, which is the greatest of all.

—Book of Mormon, Moroni 7:46

Each of us has more opportunities to do good and to be good than we ever use.

—Spencer W. Kimball (1895–1985)

We must cherish one another, watch over one another, comfort one another and gain instruction that we may all sit down in heaven together.

—Lucy Mack Smith (1775–1856)

One can never tell what will be the result of faithful service rendered, nor do we know when it will come back to us or to those with whom we are associated. The reward may not come at the time, but in dividends later. I believe we will never lose anything in life by giving service, by making sacrifices, and doing the right thing.
        —Heber J. Grant (1856–1945)

The best cure for weariness is the challenge of helping someone who is even more tired. One of the great ironies of life is this: He or she who serves almost always benefits more than he or she who is served.
        —Gordon B. Hinckley (1910–2008)

Service to others deepens and sweetens this life while we are preparing to live in a better world. It is by serving that we learn to serve. When we are engaged in the service of our fellowmen, not only do our deeds assist them, but we put our own problems in a fresher perspective. When we concern ourselves more with others, there is less time to be concerned with ourselves! In the midst of the miracle of serving, there is the promise of Jesus that by losing ourselves, we find ourselves!

—Spencer W. Kimball (1895–1985)

You can retire from a job, but don't ever retire from making extremely meaningful contributions in life.

—Stephen R. Covey (1932–2012)

A man filled with the love of God is not content with blessing his family alone, but ranges through the whole world, anxious to bless the whole human race.

—Joseph Smith (1805–1844)

Indolent and unworthy the beggar may be—but that is not your concern. It is better, said Joseph Smith, to feed ten impostors than to run the risk of turning away one honest petition.

—Hugh Nibley (1910–2005)

It is easy to give to our own, those whom we love. Their gladness becomes our joy. We are not quite so ready to give to others, even if they are in need, for their happiness does not seem so necessary to our happiness. It appears yet more difficult to give to the Lord, for we are prone to believe that he must give and ask nothing in return. We have foolishly reversed the proper order. Our first gift at Christmas should be to the Lord; next to the friend or stranger by our gate; then, surcharged with the effulgence from such giving, we would enhance the value of our gifts to our very own.

—John A. Widtsoe (1872–1952)

Sometimes we get discouraged because the needs in the world around us seem so great and our resources seem so few. We think, "We're not doing enough. We can't do enough. Nobody could do enough." When we think like that, we focus on what is left undone, and we lose the joy that comes with service. I want to tell you that we don't need to compare ourselves to anyone else, either collectively or as individuals. . . . We can do great good when we work as a united sisterhood, as long as we don't burden ourselves with unrealistic expectations that rob us of the joy of achievement.

—Chieko N. Okazaki (1926–2011)

We love no one unless we sacrifice for him. We can measure the degree of love that we possess for any man or cause, by the sacrifice we make for him or it.

—John A. Widtsoe (1872–1952)

In life all must choose at times. Sometimes, two possibilities are good; neither is evil. Usually, however, one is of greater import than the other. When in doubt, each must choose that which concerns the good of others—the greater law—rather than that which chiefly benefits ourselves—the lesser law.

—John A. Widtsoe (1872–1952)

God does not begin by asking our ability, only our availability, and if we prove our dependability, he will increase our capability.

—Neal A. Maxwell (1926–2004)

At the final day, the Savior will not ask about the nature of our callings. He will not inquire about our material possessions or fame. He will ask if we ministered to the sick, gave food and drink to the hungry, visited those in prison, or gave succor to the weak.

—Joseph B. Wirthlin (1917–2008)

When ye are in the service of your fellow beings ye are only in the service of your God.

—Book of Mormon, Mosiah 2:17

HOPE & OPTIMISM

If calling the glass half-empty is pessimism, and declaring it half-full is optimism, then hope might consist in saying, "Even if the glass is empty now, it can be full again."

For Mormons, no matter how tragic or trying a circumstance, hope and comfort can be found if one remembers that this life is only a very small portion of a greater and grander eternal plan (see **Trials** and **Purpose of Life**). Latter-day Saints believe that whether in this life or the next, all those who turn to God and repent of their sins may have all their pain eased—all sickness healed, all sorrow assuaged, all inequities erased, all wrongs righted, and all transgressions forgiven.

Does this mean that members of the LDS are always cheery and never depressed? That they always have a positive outlook on life and never despair? Of course not. But where much of the world might insist that people never change, Mormonism boldly proclaims that by the power of Christ's atonement, every man and every woman can become better than he or she was the day before (see **Repentance & Forgiveness** and **Persistence & Improvement**).

—⁓—

Search diligently, pray always, and be believing, and all things shall work together for your good.
—Doctrine & Covenants 90:24

Live life well today. Life passes quickly. Let us not be guilty of hoping that someday we will become happy and contented, after college or after this next semester or after this next test or after this date tonight or after the bills are paid or after the kids are grown or when we are retired.
—Hugh W. Pinnock (1934–2000)

The good will always outweigh the bad. . . . There are far more lovely, fine, honest people in this world than those who are dishonest and injurious.
—Hugh W. Pinnock (1934–2000)

The one who confidently looks forward to an eternal reward for his efforts in mortality is constantly sustained through his deepest trials. When he is disappointed in love, he does not commit suicide. When loved ones die, he doesn't despair; when he loses a coveted contest, he doesn't falter; when war and destruction dissipate his future, he doesn't sink into a depression. He lives above his world and never loses sight of the goal of his salvation.

—Harold B. Lee (1899–1973)

We're warned against lightmindedness. . . . But the Lord nowhere condemns lightheartedness.

—Truman G. Madsen (1926–2009)

Fear is the devil's first and chief tool.

—John A. Widtsoe (1872–1952)

O timid one, awaken, exert yourself, draw back the curtains your training and background have hung over the windows of your soul!
—Spencer W. Kimball (1895–1985)

Hope helps us to walk by faith, not by sight. This can actually be safer. When unaided spiritually, natural sight often shrinks from the odds. It is immobilized by improbabilities. Mauled by his moods and intimidated by his fears, the natural man overreacts to, while hope overrides, the disappointments of the day.
—Neal A. Maxwell (1926–2004)

Those of little faith mistake local cloud cover for general darkness. Keeping spiritually intact results in our keeping precious perspective by seeing "things as they really are" (Book of Mormon, Jacob 4:13).
—Neal A. Maxwell (1926–2004)

Everybody in this life has their challenges and difficulties. That is part of our mortal test. The reason for some of these trials cannot be readily understood except on the basis of faith and hope because there is often a larger purpose which we do not always understand. Peace comes through hope.

—James E. Faust (1920–2007)

We must not lose hope. Hope is an anchor to the souls of men. Satan would have us cast away that anchor. In this way he can bring discouragement and surrender. But we must not lose hope. . . . Though we may see that we have far to go on the road to perfection, we must not give up hope.

—Ezra Taft Benson (1899–1994)

Daily hope is vital. . . . Those with true hope often see their personal circumstances shaken, like kaleidoscopes, again and again. Yet with the "eye of faith," they still see divine pattern and purpose.

—Neal A. Maxwell (1926–2004)

Let us rejoice daily for little seasons of time in the good things we do and of which we are a part. Doing this influences our entire approach to life and can greatly affect our outlook.

—Jack H. Goaslind (1928–2011)

I am asking that we stop seeking out the storms of life and enjoy the sunlight. I am suggesting that as we go through life, we "accentuate the positive." I am asking that we look a little deeper for the good, that we still our voices of insult and sarcasm, that we more generously compliment virtue and effort.

—Gordon B. Hinckley (1910–2008)

Wherefore, whoso believeth in God might with surety hope for a better world, yea, even a place at the right hand of God, which hope cometh of faith, maketh an anchor to the souls of men, which would make them sure and steadfast, always abounding in good works, being led to glorify God.

—Book of Mormon, Ether 12:4

I should never get discouraged, whatever difficulties should surround me. If I was sunk in the lowest pit of Nova Scotia and all the Rocky Mountains piled on top of me, I ought not to be discouraged but hang on, exercise faith and keep up good courage and I should come out on the top of the heap.

—Joseph Smith (1805–1844)

The only way to get through life is to laugh your way through it. You either have to laugh or cry. I prefer to laugh. Crying gives me a head-ache.

—Marjorie Pay Hinckley (1911–2004)

Hope is trust in God's promises, faith that if we act now, the desired blessings will be fulfilled in the future.

—James E. Faust (1920–2007)

Wherefore, if a man have faith he must needs have hope; for without faith there cannot be any hope.

—Book of Mormon, Moroni 7:42

HAPPINESS

Just about everyone wants to be happy. So why do so few of us seem to achieve it? Many people spend much of their lives feeling miserable, depressed, or dissatisfied, with only fleeting moments of joy or pleasure (see **Trials**).

Mormons, like many members of other faiths, believe that happiness is one of the primary pursuits and purposes of life. Mormon doctrine teaches that God placed us on Earth, among other reasons, so that we can come to know a fullness of joy (see **Purpose of Life**). However, those who attempt to find such joy in pursuing the pleasures and priorities of this world are likely to be disappointed, for true, lasting happiness can come only from a life lived in accordance with God's will.

Mormons recognize the need for healthy amounts of rest, relaxation, and appropriate creature comforts (see **Recreation**). However, in the Mormon view, focusing on these things as the source of happiness means that we can never learn the meaning of real joy.

—⁓—

[God] never will institute an ordinance or give a commandment to his people that is not calculated in its nature to promote that happiness which he has designed, and which will not end in the greatest amount of good and glory to those who become the recipients of his law and ordinances.

—Joseph Smith (1805–1844)

Happiness is the object and design of our existence; and will be the end thereof, if we pursue the path that leads to it; and this path is virtue, uprightness, faithfulness, holiness, and keeping all the commandments of God.

—Joseph Smith (1805–1844)

I could see that in the gospel of Christ there was true happiness and true enjoyment.

—Patience Loader Rozsa Archer (1827–1921)

May we never let the things we can't have, or don't have, or shouldn't have, spoil our enjoyment of the things we do have and can have. As we value our happiness let us not forget it, for one of the greatest lessons in life is learning to be happy without the things we cannot or should not have.

—Richard L. Evans (1906–1971)

A grateful heart is a beginning of greatness. It is an expression of humility. It is a foundation for the development of such virtues as prayer, faith, courage, contentment, happiness, love, and well-being.

—James E. Faust (1920–2007)

God loves us; the devil hates us. God wants us to have a fulness of joy as he has. The devil wants us to be miserable as he is. God gives us commandments to bless us. The devil would have us break these commandments to curse us.

—Ezra Taft Benson (1899–1994)

God designs that we should enjoy ourselves. I do not believe in a religion that makes people gloomy, melancholy, miserable and ascetic. . . . I should not think there was anything great or good associated with that, while everything around, the trees, birds, flowers and green fields, were so pleasing, the insects and bees buzzing and fluttering, the lambs frolicking and playing. While everything else enjoyed life, why should not we?

—John Taylor (1808–1887)

When you find yourselves a little gloomy, look around you and find somebody that is in a worse plight than yourself; go to him and find out what the trouble is, then try to remove it with the wisdom which the Lord bestows upon you; and the first thing you know, your gloom is gone, you feel light, the Spirit of the Lord is upon you, and everything seems illuminated.

—Lorenzo Snow (1814–1901)

The pathway of righteousness is the highway of happiness. There is no other way to happiness.

—George Albert Smith (1870–1951)

When a person is miserable, wretched, and unhappy in himself, put him in what circumstances you please, and he is wretched still. If a person is poor, and composes his mind, and calmly submits to the providences of God, he will feel cheerful and happy in all circumstances, if he continues to keep the commandments of God.

—Heber C. Kimball (1801–1868)

The Lord, in his kindness, seeing the attitude of his children, and knowing that they would need guidance, gave to us the Ten Commandments, and other commandments that have been given from time to time, to help us to find happiness. You observe people running to and fro in the world, seeking happiness but not finding it. If they would only pause long enough to accept the Lord's advice happiness would follow, but they will find it in no other way.

—George Albert Smith (1870–1951)

Happiness consists not of having, but of being; not of possessing, but of enjoying. It is a warm glow of the heart at peace with itself. A martyr at the stake may have happiness that a king on his throne might envy. Man is the creator of his own happiness. It is the aroma of life, lived in harmony with high ideals. For what a man has he may be dependent upon others; what he is rests with him alone.

—David O. McKay (1873–1970)

Happiness does not depend on what happens outside of you, but what happens inside of you.
—Harold B. Lee (1899–1973)

The Lord's way builds individual self-esteem and develops and heals the dignity of the individual, whereas the world's way depresses the individual's view of himself and causes deep resentment.
—Spencer W. Kimball (1895–1985)

Life is to be enjoyed, not just endured.
—Gordon B. Hinckley (1910–2008)

I have reached out my hand, I have plucked the fruits of the Gospel, I have eaten of them, and they are sweet, yea, above all that is sweet.
—Heber J. Grant (1856–1945)

Generally speaking, the most miserable people I know are those who are obsessed with themselves; the happiest people I know are those who lose themselves in the service of others. . . . By and large, I have come to see that if we complain about life, it is because we are thinking only of ourselves.

—Gordon B. Hinckley (1910–2008)

The way to be happy is to have a conscience void of offence. Do not do any thing that will bring you into bondage under sin. . . . Learn well the short lesson to say, "No."

—Abigail Smith Abbott (1806–1889)

Adam fell that men might be; and men are, that they might have joy.

—Book of Mormon, 2 Nephi 2:25

Wickedness never was happiness.

—Book of Mormon, Alma 41:10

Abigail Smith Abbott (1806–1889) and her husband were baptized by Mormon missionaries in about 1839. The mother of eight, Abigail endured hardships in caring for her family and others after the death of her first husband and while her second husband was serving in the Mormon Battalion and on missions for the LDS Church.

Ann Marsh Abbott (1797–1849) and her husband joined the LDS Church in 1830, the year of its organization. Together with other Latter-day Saints, they endured persecution and were driven from their homes in Missouri and Illinois. They remained faithful when others around them left the Church, including her brother Thomas B. Marsh, who had introduced them to Mormonism.

Patience Loader Rozsa Archer (1827–1921) was born in England, where she and her family joined the LDS Church. In 1855, they traveled to Utah as part of the ill-fated Martin Handcart Company. Her first husband died while she was pregnant with their fourth child. She spent the last decades of her life in Pleasant Grove, Utah, where she served as a president of the local LDS Church female Relief Society.

Marvin J. Ashton (1915–1994) served as a member of the LDS Church's Quorum of the Twelve Apostles from 1971 until his death. During his career, he worked as managing director of LDS Social Services, served as a Utah state senator, and was president of Deseret Book.

Ezra Taft Benson (1899–1994) was the LDS Church's thirteenth president, serving from 1985 until his death. He was also an agricultural economist. During both presidential terms of Dwight D. Eisenhower, Benson served as the U.S. Secretary of Agriculture.

Elaine A. Cannon (1922–2003) served as the eighth general president of the LDS Church's Young Women organization. She worked as a newspaper editor, published articles in national magazines such as *Seventeen* and *Better Homes and Gardens*, and authored more than fifty books.

Joseph J. Cannon (1877–1945) was a politician, businessman, and managing editor of the *Deseret News*. He had a strong interest in literature and served as vice-president of the Theater's Guild in Salt Lake City. He presided over the LDS Church's British Mission and Temple Square Mission and served on the general board of the Young Men's Mutual Improvement Association (YMMIA).

J. Reuben Clark (1871–1961) was a counselor in the LDS Church's First Presidency from 1934 until his death, serving with three Church presidents. After earning a law degree at Columbia University, he served as Under Secretary of State for U.S. president Calvin Coolidge and was appointed as the U.S. ambassador to Mexico.

Rudger Clawson (1857–1943) began serving in the LDS Church's Quorum of the Twelve Apostles in 1898. In 1921, he became President of the Quorum. After the U.S. Congress passed the Edmunds Act, he became the first practicing polygamist to be convicted and sentenced to prison, in 1882.

Hannah Last Cornaby (1822–1905) and her husband Samuel converted to the LDS Church in 1852. Shortly afterward, they traveled from their home in England to Utah, where they helped to settle Spanish Fork. The mother of seven, she wrote the words to the hymn, "Who's on the Lord's Side?"

Stephen R. Covey (1932–2012) was a well-known author, educator, businessman, and speaker. His most popular book was *The Seven Habits of Highly Effective People*. At the time of his death, he was serving as a professor at Utah State University's Jon M. Huntsman School of Business.

Richard L. Evans (1906–1971) was a member of the LDS Church's Quorum of the Twelve Apostles from 1953 until his death. He served as president of Rotary International from 1966 to 1967. For forty-one years, he wrote, produced, and announced *Music and the Spoken Word*, the weekly Mormon Tabernacle Choir broadcast.

James E. Faust (1920–2007) served as an Assistant to the LDS Church's Quorum of the Twelve Apostles, as a member of the First Quorum of the Seventy, and as an apostle. From 1995 until his death, he served as a counselor in the First Presidency with President Gordon B. Hinckley. By profession, he was a lawyer and politician.

Jack H. Goaslind (1928–2011) became a member of the LDS Church's First Quorum of the Seventy in 1978. From 1990 to 1998, he served as general president of the LDS Young Men organization. The Boy Scouts of America awarded him the Silver Buffalo Award in 1995.

Heber J. Grant (1856–1945) was the seventh president of the LDS Church, serving from 1918 until his death. He instituted the Church's welfare program and started requiring observance of the Word of Wisdom for temple attendance. He was ordained an apostle in 1882. By profession, he was involved in banking, insurance, and politics.

Drusilla Dorris Hendricks (1810–1881) and her husband James joined the LDS Church in 1835. James was paralyzed during the persecution of the Latter-day Saints in Missouri. They moved to the Salt Lake Valley in 1847 and eventually settled in Cache Valley. They had five children.

Bryant S. Hinckley (1867–1961) was the father of LDS Church president Gordon B. Hinckley.

Known as an author and orator, he was involved in the Young Men's Mutual Improvement Association, the *Improvement Era* magazine, LDS Business College, and the Church Board of Education. He served as a stake president and mission president.

Gordon B. Hinckley (1910–2008) served as the LDS Church's fifteenth president from 1995 until his death. He was known for building temples and establishing the Perpetual Education Fund. During his presidency, the Church issued *The Family: A Proclamation to the World*. He was the author of several books.

Marjorie Pay Hinckley (1911–2004) was the wife of Church president Gordon B. Hinckley and the mother of five children. Her books and pamphlets include *Small and Simple Things* and *To Women: Is This What I Was Born to Do?* She was known for her public speaking, her sense of humor, and her devotion to family history research.

Howard W. Hunter (1907–1995) was the LDS Church's fourteenth president. He served for only nine months, the shortest tenure in the Church's history. He became an apostle at the age of fifty-one and served as a General Authority for more than thirty-five years. He was a banker and a lawyer by profession.

Orson Hyde (1805–1878) was a member of the LDS Church's original Quorum of the Twelve Apostles. From 1847 to 1875, he served as President of the Quorum of the Twelve Apostles. He served missions for the Church in the United States, Europe, and the Middle East.

Jane Elizabeth Manning James (1822–1908), a daughter of former slaves, was baptized in 1842 as one of the LDS Church's first black converts. For a time, she lived in the home of LDS founder Joseph Smith. The mother of eight, she moved to Utah and worked as a laundress and soap maker. Her life has been portrayed in a documentary, a play, and as part of a novel trilogy.

Ann Prior Jarvis (1829–1913) grew up in London, where LDS missionaries converted her and her husband. After multiple trials, they succeeded in traveling to Utah; six weeks after their arrival, Ann gave birth to their eighth child (out of eleven). The family settled in St. George, Utah, where they helped build the St. George Temple and Tabernacle.

Mary Minerva Dart Judd (1838–1909) and her family joined the westward LDS migration when she was only eleven. At fourteen, she married. She and her husband helped in the Mormon settlement of southern Utah and Nevada. They had fourteen children, many of whom died prematurely, and they adopted three Native American children. She was a midwife and often helped the sick.

Camilla Eyring Kimball (1894–1987) was the wife of Church president Spencer W. Kimball and the mother of four children. She was born in the LDS colony at Colonia Juárez, Chihuahua, Mexico. Her 1982 biography, *Camilla*, includes many of her own words. She worked as a schoolteacher and freelance newspaper reporter.

Heber C. Kimball (1801–1868) served as one of the LDS Church's original twelve apostles. In 1837, he was called to lead the first group of LDS missionaries to England, where thousands were converted. From 1847 until his death, he was first counselor to Brigham Young in the First Presidency. He was trained as a blacksmith and potter.

Spencer W. Kimball (1895–1985) was the LDS Church's twelfth president, serving from 1978 until his death. Under his leadership, in 1978 the Church ended its ban on priesthood ordination and temple ordinances for members of black African descent. Before serving the Church full time, he worked in banking and insurance.

James A. Langton (1861–1943) was a teacher and principal in Utah and Idaho before joining the staff of the *Deseret News*, where he eventually became editor. He served six years on the Utah Board of Education.

Harold B. Lee (1899–1973) served as the LDS Church's eleventh president from July 1972 until his death less than two years later. Ordained an apostle in 1941, he was a counselor in the First Presidency to Joseph Fielding Smith. During the Great Depression, he led the creation of the Church's welfare program. By profession, he was an educator and businessman, and he was also active in politics.

Truman G. Madsen (1926–2009) was a professor of religion and philosophy at Brigham Young University. His writings included *Four Essays on Love*, a paper titled *Are Christians Mormon?* and a biography of LDS historian and politician B. H. Roberts. He earned his Ph.D. at Harvard University.

J. Willard Marriott (1900–1985) was an entrepreneur who founded the Marriott Corporation. At the time of his death, the company operated 1,400 restaurants and 143 hotels and resorts worldwide, earned $4.5 billion in annual revenue, and employed 154,600 employees.

Neal A. Maxwell (1926–2004) served in the LDS Church's Quorum of the Twelve Apostles from 1981 until his death. He authored thirty books on religious themes and wrote many articles on politics and government for local, professional, and national publications. By profession, he was a university professor and administrator.

Bruce R. McConkie (1915–1985) was called to the LDS Church's First Council of the Seventy in 1946 and to the Quorum of the Twelve Apostles in 1972. He authored several doctrinal books and articles. He wrote the chapter headings for the Church's scripture editions published from 1979 to 1981. He was a lawyer by profession.

David O. McKay (1873–1970) served as the LDS Church's ninth president from 1951 until his death. Ordained an apostle in 1906 at age thirty-two, he was a General Authority for nearly sixty-four years.

He served as a counselor in the First Presidency to Heber J. Grant and George Albert Smith. He was an educator by profession.

Keith Meservy (1924–2008) taught in the Ancient Scripture Department at Brigham Young University. He was in the Army during World War II and served in the LDS Church's Northern States Mission.

George Q. Morris (1874–1962) was a member of the LDS Church's Quorum of the Twelve Apostles from 1954 until his death. He served a mission to Great Britain from 1899 until 1902. He was set apart as a president in the Second Quorum of Seventy in 1904. From 1948 to 1951, he served as president of the Eastern States Mission.

Hugh Nibley (1910–2005) was a professor of scripture at Brigham Young University. He was known as one of Mormonism's most influential scholars and apologists. Skilled in many languages, he wrote and lectured on a wide variety of scriptural and doctrinal topics. Nineteen volumes of his collected works have been published.

Stella Harris Oaks (1906–1980) was the mother of three young children when her husband died in 1940. She returned to teaching to support her family, ultimately earning a master's degree from Columbia University. She founded an adult-education program in Provo, Utah, and served for many years on the city council and as assistant mayor.

Chieko N. Okazaki (1926–2011) served as first counselor in the LDS Church's Relief Society general presidency from 1990 to 1997. After growing up Buddhist in Hawaii, she converted to Mormonism at age fifteen. An educator by profession, she authored several books and articles.

Carol Clark Ottesen (1930–2006) taught writing at California State University, Los Angeles Harbor College, and Brigham Young University. For two years, she and her husband taught English in the People's Republic of China. She was an author and poet.

Hugh W. Pinnock (1934–2000) served as an LDS Church general authority from 1977 until his death. He was a member of the First Quorum of the Seventy, and served as general president of the Sunday school from 1979 to 1986 and again from 1989 to

1992. He served in the Presidency of the Seventy from 1986 to 1989.

Parley P. Pratt (1807–1857) was a member of the LDS Church's original Quorum of the Twelve Apostles. He was a well-known author of influential books, pamphlets, poetry, and other works, for a total of thirty-one publications. He also edited two LDS periodicals. His autobiography, which remains widely read, was published posthumously.

Naomi W. Randall (1908–2001) was a songwriter, author, and leader in the LDS Church's Primary auxiliary for children. Her 1957 song "I Am a Child of God" has been published in more than ninety languages. She served on the Primary general board for twenty-seven years and in the Primary general presidency from 1970 to 1974.

Marion G. Romney (1897–1988) was called as an LDS Church apostle in 1951. He grew up in the LDS settlement of Colonia Juárez, Chihuahua, Mexico. He served as a counselor in the First Presidency with presidents Harold B. Lee and Spencer W. Kimball. By profession, he was a lawyer, and he was active in politics.

Sterling W. Sill (1903–1994) served as an Assistant to the LDS Church's Quorum of the Twelve Apostles from 1954 to 1976 and as a member of the First Quorum of the Seventy from 1976 to 1978. He wrote dozens of religious and self-improvement books and participated in radio broadcasts. He worked in the insurance industry.

Emma Hale Smith (1804–1879) was the first wife of LDS Church organizer Joseph Smith. She selected the hymns for the Church's first hymnal. In 1842, she became the first president of the Ladies' Relief Society of Nauvoo. She did not move west with the Latter-day Saint pioneers led by Brigham Young.

Barbara B. Smith (1922–2010) was the tenth general president of the LDS Church's Relief Society organization for women. She was known for opposing the proposed Equal Rights Amendment to the U.S. Constitution, the recruitment of women into the U.S. military, and abortion. She was the mother of seven children.

George A. Smith (1817–1875) was ordained to the LDS Church's Quorum of the Twelve Apostles in 1839. In 1868, he became first counselor in the

First Presidency, serving until his death. He was a cousin of Church founder Joseph Smith. The city of St. George, Utah, is named after him.

George Albert Smith (1870–1951) served as the LDS Church's eighth president from 1945 until his death. He was called as a member of the Quorum of the Twelve Apostles in 1903. He was known for his American patriotism and his support of the Boy Scouts. He was the grandson of George A. Smith (1817–1875).

Joseph F. Smith (1838–1919) was the sixth president of the LDS Church, serving from 1901 until his death. He was the last Church president to have personally known Church founder Joseph Smith. His father, Hyrum Smith, was Joseph's brother. During his career, he was a clerk and a member of the Utah Territorial Legislature.

Joseph Fielding Smith (1876–1972) served as the tenth president of the LDS Church, from 1970 until his death a short time later. He was known as a religious scholar and author. He was the son of Joseph F. Smith, sixth president of the Church. His grandfather was Hyrum Smith, brother of Church founder Joseph Smith.

Joseph Smith (1805–1844) organized the LDS Church and led it until his martyrdom. He received numerous revelations and scriptures, including the Book of Mormon, the Pearl of Great Price, and nearly all of the Doctrine & Covenants. Mormons believe that he "has done more, save Jesus only, for the salvation of men in this world, than any other man that ever lived in it" (D&C 135:3).

Lucy Mack Smith (1775–1856) was the mother of LDS Church organizer Joseph Smith. Her memoir, *Biographical Sketches of Joseph Smith, the Prophet, and His Progenitors for Many Generations*, is an important source of Church history. When the Latter-day Saints migrated to Utah, she stayed in Illinois with her daughter-in-law, Emma Hale Smith.

Eliza R. Snow (1804–1877) was an influential poet, writer, historian, and leader in nineteenth-century Mormonism. She was LDS founder Joseph Smith's plural wife and later became a plural wife of Brigham Young, the Church's second president. From 1866 until her death, she served as the second general president of the Relief Society. She was the sister of Lorenzo Snow, the Church's fifth president.

Erastus Snow (1818–1888) became a member of the LDS Church's Quorum of the Twelve Apostles in 1849. He performed missionary work in Scandinavia and in the Midwest and East of the United States. He played a lead role in establishing Mormon colonies in Arizona, Colorado, and New Mexico.

Lorenzo Snow (1814–1901) was the LDS Church's fifth president, serving from 1898 until his death. He was called to the LDS Church's Quorum of the Twelve Apostles in 1849. From 1873 to 1877, he served as a counselor to Brigham Young in the First Presidency. During his career, he helped lead colonization efforts and was involved in Utah Territory politics.

Belle S. Spafford (1895–1982) served as the ninth general president of the LDS Church's Relief Society women's organization from 1945 until 1974. During her service under six Church presidents, from Heber J. Grant to Spencer W. Kimball, the organization grew from about 100,000 members to more than one million worldwide.

N. Eldon Tanner (1898–1982) served as a counselor in the First Presidency to four LDS Church presidents, from David O. McKay through Spencer W. Kimball. He became an apostle in 1962. He was an educator and businessman, was active in the oil industry, and held several elected and appointed offices in the Canadian province of Alberta.

John Taylor (1808–1887) was the LDS Church's third president, serving from 1880 until his death. He was called to the Quorum of the Twelve Apostles in 1838. A native of England, he was the only Church president born outside of the United States. He joined the Church while living in Canada. While an apostle, he was responsible for compiling the Pearl of Great Price, one of the LDS Church's volumes of scripture.

Emma Lou Thayne (1924–2014) was an LDS poet and novelist. She also contributed to magazines and published personal essays and a biography. She wrote the hymn "Where Can I Turn for Peace?" The mother of five, she taught English at the University of Utah. She was a member of the *Deseret News* executive board for almost twenty years.

Emmeline B. Wells (1828–1921) served as the fifth general president of the LDS Church's Relief Society organization for women. Called in 1910 at age eighty-two, she served until her death. For thirty-seven years, she edited Utah's influential *Woman's Exponent* periodical. She also worked as a journalist, poet, and women's rights advocate.

John A. Widtsoe (1872–1952) was a member of the LDS Church's Quorum of the Twelve Apostles from 1921 until his death. Born in Norway, he became well known as an author, scientist, and academic. He graduated with honors from Harvard University in 1894.

Clarissa Smith Williams (1859–1930) was the sixth general president of the LDS Church's Relief Society organization for women, from 1921 to 1928. She was the mother of eleven children.

Joseph B. Wirthlin (1917–2008) became a member of the LDS Church's Quorum of the Twelve Apostles in 1986. Ten years earlier, he was called to the First Quorum of the Seventy, later serving in the quorum presidency. In 1975, he began serving as an Assistant to the Quorum of the Twelve Apostles. His career was in business.

Wilford Woodruff (1807–1898) was the fourth president of the LDS Church, serving from 1889 until his death. In 1890, he issued a manifesto that ended the practice of plural marriage among Church members. He joined the faith in 1833 and became an apostle in 1839.

Levi Edgar Young (1874–1963) was called to the LDS Church's First Council of the Seventy in 1909. He served as senior president of the Seventy from 1941 until his death. An academic by profession, he did graduate studies at Harvard University and earned an M.A. and Ph.D. in history from Columbia University.

Brigham Young (1801–1877) became president of the LDS Church after the martyrdom of founding prophet Joseph Smith, serving from 1847 until his death. He led the Mormon exodus west. He founded Salt Lake City and served as the Utah Territory's first governor. He was known as the "American Moses" and as the "Lion of the Lord."

Zina D. H. Young (1821–1901) served as the third general president of the LDS Church's Relief Society organization for women, from 1888 until her death. She was a plural wife of Joseph Smith and later of Brigham Young. She worked as a teacher, midwife, and hospital administrator and was active in the women's suffrage movement.